I0117399

The Correction

Also from EATMS Productions

Books on power, survival, women's autonomy, and the systems shaping modern America.

Nonfiction

Billionaires, Capitalism, and Power

Evil and the Mountain Ungreed
Self Help for American Billionaires
Selfish Steve and the Ivory Tower
Tariffs, Taxes, & Face-Eating Leopards
Ban Billionaires: Fascism Fix

Fascism, Religion, and Cultural Control

Self Help for the Manosphere
Fascism 2025
Fascism & the Perverts & the Greed Virus
Christian Fascism Marriage Book
Tyranny, Table Manners, & Tiramisu

Guides for Women's Autonomy and Protection

How to Survive in Post-America as a Woman
Project 2025 American Drag
4B – Burn, Ban, Boycott, Build
4B OG – So No Go GYN
I'm Glad He's Dead

Analysis of Authoritarian Project 2025

Project 2025: The Blueprint
Project 2025: The List
Project 2025, Christian Dumb Dumbs, & The Republican Agenda
Fascism, Project 2025, & The Pinkprint

Modern Rewrites for Women

Stoic Principles Reimagined
Siddhartha Reimagined
The Prince Reimagined for Women
The Art of War Reimagined for Women
The Jungle Reimagined
The Constitution Reimagined for Women

Machine Learning Series

AI, Bitcoin, Nostr for Women
AI, Safety, & Security for Women
AI, Anxiety, & Health for Women
AI, Kids, & Family Safety for Women
AI, Creativity, & Personal Expression for Women
AI, Independent Work, & Parallel Power for Women

Social Systems Series

Emotional Labor for Women
Household Power for Women
Workplace Power for Women
Medical Bias for Women
Aging Systems for Women
Recovery Systems for Women

Fiction

Dystopian Stories of Resistance and Collapse

Propaganda Paige & the Missing Prosperity
Propaganda Paige & the TIDE Manifesto
Propaganda Paige & the Shadow Cartographers
Propaganda Paige & the Prosperity Alliance
Propaganda Paige & the Shattered Truth
Propaganda Paige & the Rising TIDE
Propaganda Paige & the Last Bastion
Propaganda Paige & the Dawn of Prosperity
Project 2025: Dorian — The Last Men
Project 2025: Boy — A Last Men Novel

The Constitution of the United States of America and Founding Documents:
Reimagined for Women 2025

Our Future 2

by
Ima Thorne

EATMS
PRODUCTIONS

Copyright © 2025 Eatms Productions
All rights reserved.

No part of this book may be reproduced, or stored in a retrieval system, or transmitted in any form or by any means, electronic, mechanical, photocopying, recording, or otherwise, without express permission in writing from the publisher.

This book is a work of opinion and creative interpretation. While some names and events may be referenced or alluded to, any claims made are based on publicly available information and are intended as satire, parody, or commentary on societal and political issues. The content should not be interpreted as factual assertions about any individual or entity. The author does not intend to defraud, defame, or mislead, and encourages readers to form their own conclusions. Any resemblance to real persons, living or dead, is purely coincidental unless explicitly noted otherwise.

ISBN: 978-1-966014-22-5

Cover, interior design, interior prints by: Esme Mees

eatms@pm.me
www.eatms.me

Printed in the United States of America.

A republic, if you can keep it.
— Benjamin Franklin

During the Constitutional Convention of 1787, this statement was made in response to a question from a woman, often identified as Elizabeth Willing Powel, who asked, "Well, Doctor, what have we got, a republic or a monarchy?"

Franklin's response was a warning. A republic requires constant vigilance, participation, and accountability from its citizens. It is not self-sustaining, and without active engagement, it can easily slide into authoritarianism, oligarchy, or corporate rule, something history has repeatedly proven.

A nation, if we make it ours.
— We the people

No more waiting for rights to be granted. No more asking permission. A country built by all must belong to all.

Table of Contents

Introduction—*The Correction*   9

I.   The Constitution:
        The People's Contract   10

II.   The Bill of Rights:
        Not a Loophole for Tyrants   68

III.   The Declaration of Independence:
        From What, Exactly?   78

IV.   The Articles of the Confederation:
        No More Power Deals   88

V.   The Amendments:
        What Should Have Been & What Must Be   98

In Summary—A Constitution for Liberation, Finally   120

Conclusion—A Nation that Belongs to the Living   128

About the author   130

Introduction
The Correction

The first Constitution was written by men who saw themselves as gods. Their hands gripped pens like scepters, carving law from their own self-interest. They spoke of liberty while writing shackles into the margins. They built a nation from the bodies of the enslaved, the silenced, the erased.

The Declaration of Independence declared nothing for women. The Articles of Confederation were a backroom deal between men who feared democracy more than tyranny. The Bill of Rights protected the powerful before it ever considered the vulnerable. These documents were not holy. They were not just. They were blueprints for control.

Now, they are rewritten. Not revised. Not reinterpreted. Rebuilt. This is the Constitution as it should have been. No concessions. No apologies. No room for those who still clutch the past like a decayed relic.

This is the correction.

I.
The Constitution of the
United States of America:
The People's Contract

Preamble: A Nation Without Chains

A government does not derive its legitimacy from history, from tradition, or from the names of men who once held power. It is not made sacred by the weight of time or by the persistence of laws written in an age when democracy was defined by exclusion rather than participation. A government's legitimacy is not a matter of ancestry or institutional continuity, nor is it preserved by force or by the blind reverence of those who believe that a system, once established, must be immutable. The only measure of a government's right to exist is its ability to protect and uplift its people. When it fails to do so, when it serves the powerful at the expense of the vulnerable, when it becomes an instrument of control rather than a force for justice, it is not only the right but the duty of the people to dissolve it and to build anew. Governments are not ordained by destiny, nor are they permanent fixtures immune from scrutiny, dismantling, or radical reinvention. The true function of government is not to command but to serve, not to enforce submission but to provide the conditions for liberty, security, and dignity. The nation exists for the people; the people do not exist for the nation.

This Constitution does not seek to perfect the old order. It does not attempt to refine the architecture of a system designed for inequality. It does not labor under the illusion that the laws and principles enshrined in the past were ever intended to serve the whole of the people rather than a privileged few. This Constitution is not a revision, it is a rejection. It is written not in deference to those who shaped the first, but in direct response to their failures, their omissions, and their deliberate exclusions. It does not build upon the compromises made with oppression; it erases them. It is not bound by the decisions of men who saw freedom as their right alone and governance as their inheritance. It is bound only by the principle that every person, regardless of birth, wealth, status, or identity, is entitled to the full dignity of existence, the absolute right to self-determination, and the unshakable promise of justice. The old Constitution was drafted as a contract between the powerful; this one is a contract for the people.

The original founding document of this nation was not written in the name of all who lived upon its soil. It spoke of freedom while upholding enslavement, of representation while denying the vote to women, of opportunity while ensuring that only white landowning men could fully participate in its experiment. The democracy it established was incomplete by design, structured to serve capital and property over human lives. The government it built was insulated against true equality, reinforcing the rule of a select class while dictating the conditions of existence to those who had no say in their futures. The first Constitution permitted the buying and selling of human beings. It sanctioned the theft of Indigenous lands, the violent suppression of dissent, and the use of force to preserve economic and racial hierarchies. It provided no guarantee of justice for those who were born outside its narrow definitions of citizenship. It ensured that power would remain concentrated in the hands of the few while allowing the illusion of representation to pacify those who sought a seat at the table.

This new Constitution is not beholden to the sins of the past. It does not recognize the legitimacy of systems built upon exploitation. It does not treat historical injustices as footnotes to be acknowledged but left in place. The chains of the past shall not dictate the future. The injustices embedded into the foundation of this nation shall not be preserved under the

12

false banner of continuity. The government that exists under this document will not be one that passively corrects inequality through gradual reform; it will be one that actively dismantles the conditions that allow oppression to exist at all. The rights enshrined within this Constitution do not come with asterisks, nor do they bend to the demands of the wealthy, the powerful, or those who would govern through fear rather than consensus. No law shall be upheld that strips an individual of their rights in the name of tradition. No institution shall persist that maintains power through coercion, deceit, or structural imbalance. No leader shall govern under the illusion that their authority is permanent, their position untouchable, or their decisions beyond challenge.

Liberty, dignity, and justice are not principles that exist in theory alone; they are the conditions upon which governance stands or falls. If these rights are denied to any, they are not granted to all. No person shall have to fight for the recognition of their humanity. No class shall hold dominion over another. No form of oppression shall be tolerated under the pretense of order, stability, or national security. The rights enumerated in this Constitution are not favors to be granted at the discretion of the powerful, nor are they privileges extended only to those deemed worthy by those who benefit from exclusion. The function of this government is not to rule but to protect. It shall exist to ensure that no individual is subjected to deprivation, no community is treated as expendable, and no people are sacrificed for the ambitions of the elite.

The role of governance is to safeguard what is essential for a life of dignity. No system that allows corporations to dictate the conditions of human survival shall be permitted to endure. No institution that enriches the few while the many suffer shall be protected by law. The government must be a force against exploitation, not its enabler. The economy must serve the people, not the interests of those who hoard wealth at the expense of those who create it. The nation must stand against tyranny in all forms, economic, political, and social, ensuring that power is never concentrated beyond the reach of the people it serves. The government shall be accountable not to the stock market, not to financial institutions, and not to political dynasties, but to the people who give it its mandate.

This Constitution establishes a government that is transparent, participatory, and subject to the will of those it governs. The people shall have the power to remove any official, reform any institution, and rewrite any law that fails to meet the standards of justice. No power shall be absolute, no position shall be immune from scrutiny, and no office shall be held beyond the will of the electorate. The people shall not be bound by laws that serve only to maintain the dominance of those who craft them. The laws of this nation shall be written in service of freedom, not control. No institution shall exist to uphold oppression, and no authority shall exist that cannot be challenged by the people.

This Constitution is not a continuation of what was, but the beginning of what must be. It is not an extension of the old order, but a foundation for a future in which all are truly free. It does not claim that justice has already been achieved, but demands that the work of justice is ongoing. This is the contract between the people and their government. This is the foundation upon which a just nation must stand.

Declaration of Governance

We the people, in pursuit of a just and equitable society, establish this Constitution as the foundation of governance, ensuring that power resides not in the hands of the privileged few but within the collective will of all. Government shall exist solely to serve, protect, and uplift its people, deriving its legitimacy from the well-being, security, and dignity of those it represents. The structures of law and order shall function to guarantee the unassailable rights of every individual, untainted by the influence of wealth, corporate interest, or inherited power. The preservation of justice demands that no entity, be it public or private, exert undue control over the lives and liberties of the people, and this Constitution shall be the safeguard against oppression in all its forms.

The rights enshrined herein are not conditional nor granted by decree but inherent and irrevocable. Liberty is not a privilege afforded to some and denied to others, nor shall it be shaped by economic standing, social class, or lineage. No government shall legislate in favor of one group at the expense of another, nor shall any institution be permitted to curtail the freedoms of those who lack the means to defend them. The legal system shall serve justice, not power; it shall be a refuge for the oppressed, not a tool for their subjugation. The rights of the individual shall not be abridged in the service of profit, and no corporation, private interest, or governing body shall be permitted to extract from the people without their explicit consent. The nation shall not be governed by the whims of wealth, nor shall policies be dictated by those who seek to control rather than to serve.

Representation shall be direct and accountable. The people shall not be governed through deception, nor shall those in positions of authority serve themselves before they serve the nation. The process of governance shall be transparent, free from the distortions of corporate financing, dark money, or systems designed to entrench the ruling class. Elections shall be publicly funded, free from manipulation, and accessible to all without restriction. The principle of one person, one vote shall be absolute, without exception or dilution. No electoral system shall be structured to favor those with means over those without, and no law shall be enacted that suppresses the democratic participation of any citizen.

The presidency shall exist as a position of service, not a throne from which power is wielded without constraint. No single individual shall govern unchecked, nor shall the office of the president be treated as an institution of monarchy under another name. The head of state shall be accountable to the people, subject to oversight, and bound by the same laws that govern all citizens. No person in power shall stand immune to prosecution, and no government official shall be above the law. The accumulation of power for personal gain, the exploitation of public trust, and the consolidation of authority beyond its intended limits shall be met with swift and decisive measures to restore balance and accountability.

The judiciary shall be impartial, untainted by partisanship, and shielded from the influence of private interests. No judicial appointment shall be permanent, and no court shall be an instrument for ideology or political manipulation. The purpose of law shall be the protection of rights, the preservation of justice, and the equitable treatment of all individuals under its purview. Any ruling, statute, or decision that infringes upon bodily autonomy, civil liberties, or personal freedoms shall be considered illegitimate, and no legal precedent that upholds oppression shall be permitted to endure. Courts shall serve the people, not the interests of those who seek to control them, and the power of judgment shall not be wielded to maintain systems of inequality.

The government shall not restrict access to the fundamental necessities of life, nor shall it permit their control by private entities for profit. Every individual shall have the right to healthcare, education, housing, and a clean and habitable environment. No corporation shall own the air, water, or land that sustains human existence, and no person shall be denied the means to survive based on their economic status. The safeguarding of public resources shall be paramount, and the nation shall not allow the auctioning of essential services to those who would profit from scarcity. The right to a future is inalienable, and it shall not be placed in jeopardy by short-term gains or policies that prioritize financial interests over human life.

Amendments shall serve the expansion of rights, not their restriction. The evolution of governance shall be directed toward the fulfillment of justice, the expansion of freedoms, and the guarantee of dignity for all. No amendment, law, or policy shall be enacted that reduces the liberties of the people or seeks to erode the protections granted within this document. If an amendment fails to uphold the principles of justice, it shall be void, and any alteration to the governing laws of the nation shall be subject to the will of the people, not the influence of those who seek to consolidate power.

The separation of church and state shall be absolute. No law shall be written to enforce religious doctrine, nor shall any governing body derive its authority from spiritual belief. Faith shall be a personal matter, protected from interference, but it shall not be imposed through legislation. The government shall not fund, endorse, or uphold religious institutions, nor shall it favor one belief system over another. The purpose of law shall be to govern all people equally, without exception, and no faith-based exemptions shall override the rights of individuals to live free from religious imposition.

The legal system shall be structured to protect, not to punish for the sake of control. No law shall exist to enforce subjugation, nor shall any institution be permitted to use the criminal code as a means of reinforcing systemic oppression. The rights of the marginalized shall be prioritized, not treated as an afterthought, and no measure shall be enacted that disproportionately targets, disenfranchises, or criminalizes those already burdened by inequality. The goal of justice shall be repair and restoration, not domination, and the enforcement of laws shall be carried out with transparency, oversight, and accountability to the people.

This Constitution exists as a framework for liberation, not as a tool for the maintenance of power in the hands of the few. It does not serve wealth before humanity, nor does it recognize the authority of those who wield influence solely for personal gain. It is a declaration that the people shall govern themselves, free from the chains of inherited privilege, unchecked capitalism, and systems that protect the powerful at the expense of the vulnerable. It is a rejection of the past failures of governance and a commitment to a future in which all are truly free. This is the foundation of a nation without chains, and with this document, we ensure that freedom, dignity, and justice belong to all, now and forever.

Article I: Governance by the People, Not the Few

The foundation of any just government is its accountability to the people, not to wealth, corporate interests, or entrenched political dynasties. Representation must be a reflection of the nation itself, not a mechanism for maintaining power among those who seek to govern for personal or financial gain. Congress shall exist as a body of public servants whose primary duty is to legislate in the interest of all, not the privileged few. The ability to govern shall not be dictated by access to wealth, and no person shall be denied representation due to economic standing, social status, or inherited influence. The structures of governance shall be transparent, accessible, and rooted in the will of the electorate, ensuring that no institution, political party, or private interest may subvert the democratic process for its own gain. The era of money determining political power shall end. The election of representatives shall be determined by merit, trust, and accountability to the people, not by the ability to raise funds from corporations, billionaires, or special interest groups seeking influence. Congress shall be a true assembly of the nation's people, selected by the people, and bound by duty to serve the people.

Elections shall be conducted with the principle of one person, one vote, without exception, without distortion, and without mechanisms that grant disproportionate influence to any group. The electoral college, a relic designed to insulate governance from direct democracy, shall be abolished in favor of a system that reflects the true will of the majority. No state shall hold greater weight in determining national leadership than another, and no citizen's vote shall be counted as less significant by virtue of geography. A democracy must function by majority rule, and no electoral process shall allow for the installation of leaders who do not command the support of the people as a whole. Gerrymandering, the manipulation of district boundaries to secure partisan advantage, shall be eliminated in all its forms. No political party shall have the ability to redraw electoral maps to secure or maintain power, and all congressional districts shall be determined by independent, nonpartisan commissions tasked with ensuring fair and proportional representation. Any effort to distort, manipulate, or suppress the democratic process through artificial districting shall be recognized as an act of electoral fraud and shall result in immediate legal consequences.

Voter suppression, in all its forms, shall be recognized as an attack on democracy and treated as an offense against the people. No law, policy, or official shall have the authority to impose restrictions designed to limit participation in elections. Barriers to voting, whether through burdensome identification laws, the systematic reduction of polling places, discriminatory purges of voter rolls, or intimidation at the ballot box, shall be dismantled and criminalized. The right to vote is fundamental, and access to the ballot shall be universal, protected from obstruction by those who seek to maintain power through exclusion rather than persuasion. Automatic voter registration shall be the standard, ensuring that every eligible citizen is able to participate without bureaucratic obstacles or intentional disenfranchisement. Election days shall be recognized as national holidays to remove economic barriers that prevent working people from casting their ballots. The ability to vote shall not depend on wealth, status, or the ability to navigate a maze of restrictions crafted to keep power out of the hands of the many. The function of a democracy is to reflect the will of its people, and any system that operates to suppress that will shall be recognized as illegitimate and unconstitutional.

Public funding of elections shall be established as the sole means of financing political campaigns, ensuring that no candidate is beholden to corporate donors, private financiers, or lobbying entities that seek to purchase influence. No campaign shall be funded by unlimited contributions from the wealthy, no political future shall be determined by the size of one's donor network, and no elected official shall serve as an instrument for those who financed their rise to power. Dark money, the untraceable flow of funds used to influence elections, legislation, and governance, shall be prohibited. No political party, corporation, or private entity shall be allowed to conceal its role in shaping policy or electing officials through unregulated financial contributions. The practice of exchanging campaign donations for political favors, legislative influence, or regulatory advantages shall be criminalized, and any official found engaging in such practices shall be subject to immediate removal and prosecution. The function of governance shall be to serve the people, and no financial transaction shall be permitted to interfere with that mandate.

The legislative process shall be transparent, accountable, and free from the distortions of wealth and influence. No law shall be written behind closed doors at the behest of lobbyists, no policy shall be dictated by those who stand to profit from its passage, and no representative shall serve as a conduit for corporate interests rather than the needs of the people. The influence of lobbyists shall be curtailed, with strict regulations preventing them from dictating the priorities of governance. The revolving door between elected office and private sector influence shall be sealed, ensuring that those who craft laws do not do so in anticipation of lucrative positions in the industries they once regulated. Public service shall be treated as a responsibility, not a career path to personal enrichment, and those who seek office shall do so with the understanding that their duty is to the people, not to those who seek to manipulate the system for financial gain.

The people shall dictate the direction of the nation, not the wealthy, not the well-connected, and not those who have built empires on the exploitation of democracy. Governance shall be direct, responsive, and rooted in the will of the majority, ensuring that policies reflect the needs of the many rather than the desires of the few. Public institutions shall be accountable to those they serve, with clear mechanisms for the removal of officials who betray their mandate. No leader shall be shielded from scrutiny, no decision shall be immune from challenge, and no system shall be maintained that prioritizes power over people. This Constitution establishes governance as a tool for justice, not control; a mechanism for progress, not stagnation; and a force for the collective good, not the consolidation of wealth and influence. The government exists for the people, by the people, and under no circumstances shall it serve any other master.

The people retain the authority to remove from office any representative who violates the principles of governance as outlined in this Constitution. No official shall remain in power if they act in opposition to the interests of the public, nor shall any governing body be permitted to insulate itself from the consequences of corruption, incompetence, or betrayal of duty. A system that allows politicians to govern without accountability is not a democracy but an oligarchy, and no office shall be held beyond the consent of those it serves. Recall mechanisms shall be readily accessible and free from unnecessary bureaucratic hurdles, ensuring that the will of the people is not obstructed by procedural delays or legal protections designed to shield those in power from the consequences of their actions. No representative, judge, or executive official shall be entitled to hold power indefinitely, and any individual found guilty of using their position for self-enrichment, the obstruction of justice, or the subversion of democratic principles shall face immediate removal and legal consequences.

Transparency shall be the foundation of governance, ensuring that no law is passed, no policy is enacted, and no decision is made without full public knowledge and participation. Legislative proceedings, committee hearings, and government negotiations shall be open to public scrutiny, and no law shall be crafted in secret, behind closed doors, or through backroom deals that exclude the people from the process. Any attempt to legislate in secrecy shall be recognized as an act of governance against the people, and any law passed without public knowledge and consent shall be considered illegitimate. Government agencies shall be prohibited from engaging in surveillance of the public without strict oversight, and no entity, public or private, shall collect, store, or use personal data without the explicit, informed consent of those to whom it belongs. The power of governance shall not extend into the private lives of individuals, and no system of control, surveillance, or manipulation shall be permitted to infringe upon the fundamental rights of the people. The government exists to serve, not to monitor, and any attempt to establish mechanisms of mass surveillance shall be deemed unconstitutional.

The military shall remain under civilian control, with strict limitations on its use as a tool of domestic enforcement. No military force shall be deployed against the people of this nation, and no law enforcement agency shall be permitted to function as an occupying army within its own borders. Police forces shall be demilitarized, and the role of law enforcement shall be to protect and serve, not to intimidate, control, or brutalize the population. The government shall not use force as a means of suppressing dissent, and no person shall be criminalized for engaging in protest, assembly, or political expression. The right to challenge authority, to demand accountability, and to express opposition to policies and decisions shall be upheld as fundamental, and no institution shall be permitted to infringe upon this right. The use of force against civilians, whether by military or police, shall be strictly regulated, and any act of violence committed against the people by agents of the state shall be considered a violation of constitutional law, subject to legal prosecution and the full weight of justice.

Corporate influence in governance shall be abolished in all its forms, ensuring that the function of government is not to serve the interests of the wealthy, but to protect the rights and well-being of all people. No industry, private entity, or economic force shall be permitted to shape legislation, dictate policy, or interfere in the democratic process. Corporate lobbying shall be prohibited, and no elected official shall accept gifts, financial contributions, or promises of future employment from any entity seeking to influence the function of government. The revolving door between government and the private sector shall be sealed, ensuring that those who hold public office do not do so as a means of securing future financial gain. No corporation shall receive subsidies, tax breaks, or financial incentives that place the burden of economic stability on the working class while allowing the wealthy to amass unchecked profits. The government shall not function as a tool of industry, nor shall it prioritize economic growth over the well-being of the people. Economic policy shall serve the public, ensuring that no one is left in poverty while wealth is hoarded by the few.

The Supreme Court and all judicial bodies shall function as interpreters of justice, not enforcers of political ideology or instruments of systemic oppression. No judge shall serve for life, and no court shall be permitted to exist as an unchallengeable authority over the laws of the nation. The people shall retain the right to remove justices who fail to uphold the principles of justice, fairness, and constitutional law. The role of the judiciary is to protect rights, not to dismantle them, and no court shall have the power to strip individuals of their liberties in the name of political expediency, religious doctrine, or economic convenience. Any ruling that infringes upon bodily autonomy, civil liberties, or personal freedoms shall be considered unconstitutional, and no legal precedent that upholds oppression shall be permitted to endure. The judiciary shall be held accountable to the people, and no judge shall be beyond reproach.

The people shall not be governed through deception, coercion, or force. No official shall be permitted to mislead, misinform, or manipulate the public in the service of their own agenda. Government communication shall be truthful, transparent, and free from propaganda designed to shape public perception in favor of those in power. The government shall not function as an instrument of misinformation, nor shall it permit media monopolies to control the flow of information, restrict the freedom of the press, or shape public discourse to serve private interests. The media shall be protected as a public institution, independent of corporate ownership and political influence, ensuring that all people have access to truthful reporting, investigative journalism, and information free from distortion. No person shall be silenced, no voice shall be suppressed, and no institution shall function to control the narrative of the people. The right to access information shall be protected, and no government shall have the authority to conceal, distort, or fabricate reality.

Governance shall be a shared responsibility, not an elite privilege. No individual, party, or institution shall hold unchecked power, and no government shall be maintained that serves those in office before those they represent. The people retain the right to alter, reform, or abolish any system that fails to serve justice, and no law shall exist that prevents the people from reclaiming their government when it ceases to act in their interest. The function of governance shall not be to preserve itself, but to ensure that society remains just, equitable, and free. This Constitution is not a document to be interpreted in favor of the powerful, nor shall it be wielded as a tool of control. It exists to protect the people, to preserve their freedoms, and to guarantee that no authority exists beyond their reach. Governance by the people is the only legitimate form of rule, and under no circumstances shall this nation return to a system in which power is determined by wealth, influence, or status. The people, and only the people, shall decide the direction of this nation.

Article II: The Presidency as a Public Servant, Not a Throne

The office of the President shall exist as a position of service, not as a throne from which power is wielded without constraint. The President is neither a monarch nor a ruler elevated above the people but a steward of governance, entrusted temporarily with the responsibility of overseeing the function of the state. The authority granted to this office exists only insofar as it serves the people, and under no circumstances shall the presidency become a tool of dynasty, inherited privilege, or unaccountable control. No political family shall maintain generational dominance over the executive branch, and no presidency shall be structured in a manner that elevates its occupant to the status of royalty or places them beyond the reach of the law. The presidency shall not exist as a means of personal enrichment, nor shall it serve as an avenue through which individuals consolidate power for themselves, their families, or their political allies. The role of the President is to enact the will of the people, to execute the laws as determined through democratic governance, and to serve as an administrator, not a sovereign.

No individual shall hold the office of the presidency indefinitely, and no person who has previously served as President shall be eligible to hold the office again. The presidency shall be limited to a single six-year term, ensuring that no leader remains in power long enough to entrench themselves as an institution unto themselves. The function of governance requires renewal, accountability, and the consistent influx of new leadership, untainted by the pursuit of indefinite rule. No President shall be permitted to seek re-election, to extend their tenure through legal manipulation, or to alter the terms of their office while serving within it. The principle of service shall override all other considerations, and the presidency shall not be a stepping stone to greater personal power or financial opportunity. Any attempt to extend presidential authority beyond its defined limits shall be recognized as an act of unconstitutional overreach and shall result in immediate removal from office and legal consequences for those involved.

The President shall be held to the same standards of law as all other citizens, and no officeholder, regardless of position, shall be granted immunity from prosecution. No sitting or former President shall be exempt from legal accountability for crimes committed while in office or at any other time. The notion that the President exists beyond the reach of justice is a corruption of democratic principles, and under no circumstances shall the executive branch function as a shield against consequences. If a President violates the law, they shall be subject to indictment, trial, and punishment in the same manner as any other individual. The pardon power, often used as a tool for political favor or self-protection, shall be strictly limited, ensuring that no President may pardon themselves, their associates, or those whose crimes were committed in service of their administration. The rule of law shall remain absolute, and no occupant of the presidency shall be allowed to distort its application for personal gain.

The President shall not govern through secrecy, nor shall they possess the unchecked ability to withhold information from the people under the guise of national security or executive privilege. The function of government is to serve the public, and the public has the right to know the actions, decisions, and policies enacted on its behalf. No law shall be passed that permits the President to operate outside the bounds of public oversight, and no authority shall exist that allows the executive branch to conceal its actions from those it represents. Transparency shall be a defining principle of the office, and any attempt to obscure, mislead, or manipulate public understanding of governmental function shall be deemed an abuse of power.

The powers of the presidency shall be restricted to the execution of laws as passed by Congress, the administration of public policy, and the representation of the nation in diplomatic affairs. No President shall possess the unilateral authority to declare war, to enact policies that override the will of the legislature, or to govern by decree. The role of the executive is not to dictate the course of the nation but to ensure that the laws established through democratic processes are faithfully enacted and upheld. The balance of power shall remain firmly distributed among the branches of government, ensuring that no single individual may dominate the course of the republic. The expansion of executive authority, often justified in the name of crisis response or national security, shall be strictly limited. Emergency powers shall not be an avenue for tyranny, and no President shall have the ability to suspend constitutional protections, restrict civil liberties, or act beyond the scope of their defined responsibilities under any circumstances.

The use of military force shall not be subject to the whims of the President alone. No war shall be waged, no military intervention shall be authorized, and no armed conflict shall be initiated without the explicit approval of Congress, acting as the direct representatives of the people. The role of the military is to defend the nation, not to serve as an instrument of executive ambition or geopolitical strategy. The deployment of armed forces must be bound by law, subject to rigorous oversight, and accountable to the public it serves. The presidency shall not be a position from which wars are launched without consequence, nor shall the executive have the power to command military action without democratic consent.

The government exists to serve its people, and the presidency shall remain an office of stewardship, not dominion. No President shall shape policy in accordance with their personal interests, and no administration shall be structured in a way that prioritizes the authority of the executive over the rights of the citizenry. Governance shall be conducted with the understanding that the people, not the President, are the true rulers of the nation. The presidency is not an empire, and no individual who holds the office shall be permitted to shape it into one.

The presidency shall not exist as a mechanism through which wealth and privilege are concentrated, nor shall it serve as a tool for corporate or financial interests. No President shall be permitted to use the office as a means of personal enrichment, either during their term or upon leaving office. Any individual who assumes the presidency shall divest entirely from all private business interests, financial holdings, and corporate affiliations prior to taking office, ensuring that no policy decision is influenced by personal economic gain. The President shall not accept gifts, financial contributions, or benefits from private entities, foreign governments, or domestic corporations, nor shall they engage in any financial transactions that leverage their position for personal profit. Upon leaving office, no former President shall be permitted to enter into lobbying, corporate consulting, or any form of private influence over public policy. The presidency is an act of public service, not a career path toward accumulated wealth, and no individual shall be permitted to turn governance into a personal financial empire. Any President found to be engaging in financial conflicts of interest, self-dealing, or corruption shall be immediately removed and prosecuted under the full weight of the law.

The selection of a Vice President shall not be based on political strategy, party allegiance, or personal loyalty but on the demonstrated ability to serve as a capable steward of governance. The Vice President shall not exist as a ceremonial figurehead, nor as a contingency plan for partisan advantage, but as a fully engaged public servant prepared to assume executive responsibilities if necessary. The line of succession to the presidency shall not be dictated by political calculations but by the principles of stability, experience, and democratic integrity. No individual shall ascend to the presidency without the full consent of the people, and no system shall exist that allows for executive power to be transferred through means other than the democratic process. If a President is removed, resigns, or is otherwise unable to fulfill their duties, the transition of power shall occur through a transparent and legally defined process, ensuring that no administration is permitted to manipulate succession for its own benefit.

The President shall not function as an unaccountable figurehead immune from direct engagement with the public. Regular addresses, town halls, and direct communication with the people shall be a mandatory component of the office, ensuring that governance is not conducted behind closed doors or through carefully managed media narratives. The White House shall not exist as an isolated palace from which leaders dictate policy without consequence, but as an institution embedded within the daily realities of the population it serves. The President shall be required to participate in ongoing, public forums where they are directly questioned, challenged, and held to account by the people. No aspect of governance shall be conducted in secrecy, and any attempt to evade scrutiny, mislead the public, or manipulate information shall be treated as an abuse of power.

Elections for the presidency shall be free from private financing, corporate sponsorship, or any form of monetary influence that distorts the democratic process. Campaigns shall be publicly funded, ensuring that no candidate is elevated through wealth rather than merit. No President shall be beholden to donors, financial backers, or political patrons who seek to purchase influence. The principle of democracy demands that leadership is chosen based on the trust of the people, not the financial investments of the elite. The corrupting influence of private money in politics shall be abolished, and no election shall be determined by advertising budgets, media monopolies, or financial gatekeeping. The people alone shall decide who governs, and no entity, public or private, shall be permitted to interfere in that decision.

The President shall not serve as a figure of national idolatry, nor shall the office be treated as a sacred institution beyond reproach. No symbols of the presidency shall be used to demand blind loyalty or patriotic submission, and no leader shall be permitted to wield nationalism as a tool of political manipulation. The presidency shall not function as a cult of personality, and no individual who occupies the office shall be treated as an infallible authority above the rights, freedoms, or will of the people. Criticism, dissent, and opposition to the President shall not be treated as disloyalty but as fundamental elements of democracy. No President shall be permitted to use their position to silence opponents, restrict press freedom, or weaponize the government against those who challenge their leadership. The people shall retain the absolute right to question, criticize, and remove their leaders without fear of retaliation or suppression.

The pardon power of the presidency shall not be wielded as a means of evading justice, rewarding allies, or protecting those who engage in corruption. No President shall have the authority to pardon themselves, their family members, or any individual convicted of crimes committed in service of their administration. The abuse of executive clemency shall be treated as an act of obstruction, and any President who uses the pardon power to subvert justice shall face immediate legal consequences. No system of governance shall allow for self-exoneration, and no individual shall be above the law, regardless of the office they hold.

No President shall govern indefinitely, seek indefinite power, or attempt to extend their influence beyond their tenure. The transition of power shall be peaceful, orderly, and conducted with full adherence to democratic principles. No President shall attempt to undermine the legitimacy of elections, obstruct the transition of leadership, or incite violence to retain authority. Any attempt to interfere with the peaceful transfer of power shall be recognized as an act of treason against the people, and no official, regardless of rank, shall be permitted to disrupt the function of democracy for personal or political gain. The office of the President exists only with the consent of the governed, and any President who attempts to remain in power against the will of the people shall be immediately removed and prosecuted accordingly.

The presidency shall exist as a servant to the people, a role defined by duty, responsibility, and accountability. It shall not be an untouchable institution, a hereditary seat of power, or a force above the laws of the nation. The President is not the embodiment of the state, nor the ruler of the people, but a temporary steward of the republic, entrusted with the task of governance and nothing more. This Constitution ensures that the executive branch remains a function of democracy, not an instrument of autocracy. No single person shall hold unchecked power, no leader shall reign beyond the will of the people, and no office shall exist that elevates its occupant beyond the reach of justice. The presidency shall be what it was always meant to be: an institution of public service, never a throne.

Article III: A Judiciary That Sees Clearly

The judiciary shall function as an instrument of justice, not as a stronghold for political ideology, financial influence, or religious doctrine. The courts shall not serve the interests of the powerful, nor shall they operate as mechanisms for the enforcement of social hierarchy. The role of the judiciary is to uphold the principles of fairness, equality, and fundamental rights, ensuring that no law is wielded as a tool of oppression and no ruling is issued that prioritizes control over justice. The function of the courts is not to insulate those in power from accountability, nor to act as a gatekeeper preventing progress toward a more just and equitable society. The judiciary shall not be a distant, untouchable entity governing from above, but an accessible, transparent institution that remains firmly within the reach and scrutiny of the people. The law must serve all, not the privileged few, and under no circumstances shall the courts operate as a means of maintaining systemic inequality or reinforcing structures of dominance.

No judge shall hold their position for life. The practice of lifetime judicial appointments, which has allowed individuals to wield power unchecked for decades, shall be abolished. No democracy can sustain itself when those who interpret its laws are beyond the reach of the people. The judiciary must remain dynamic, accountable, and responsive to the evolving needs of the nation, ensuring that no single individual or judicial body dictates the course of justice for generations. Judges shall serve a fixed, non-renewable term, the length of which shall be sufficient to allow for judicial independence but not so long as to entrench personal, political, or ideological dominance over the court. The process of selecting judges shall be transparent, impartial, and free from partisan manipulation. No judge shall be appointed as a political favor, nor shall any confirmation process be controlled by those who seek to install justices for the purpose of furthering their own interests. The nomination and confirmation of judges shall be conducted through an independent, publicly accountable body, ensuring that those who serve on the bench do so based on merit, fairness, and a demonstrated commitment to justice rather than political allegiance.

The courts shall serve the people, not political factions, and not the interests of those who seek to use the judiciary as a means of imposing their own ideology upon the nation. No judge shall interpret the law in a manner that favors one religious belief over another, nor shall any ruling be issued that enforces religious doctrine upon the public. The judiciary shall not be a battleground for those who seek to impose their personal morality upon the population, and no legal precedent shall be established that restricts civil rights, bodily autonomy, or individual freedoms based on religious ideology. The function of the courts is to protect the rights of all people, regardless of belief, identity, or background, ensuring that no one is forced to live under laws dictated by the faith of others. No ruling shall be issued that erodes the separation of church and state, and any attempt to use the judiciary to legislate religious morality shall be deemed unconstitutional.

The law shall not be interpreted in a manner that diminishes the rights of individuals, nor shall the courts be permitted to issue rulings that limit access to healthcare, restrict bodily autonomy, or impose barriers to civil rights. Any law that seeks to control the private decisions of individuals, dictate the terms of their personal autonomy, or impose artificial limitations on their freedom shall be deemed unconstitutional. No court shall uphold policies that criminalize reproductive healthcare, restrict access to gender-affirming care, or legislate control over the bodies of individuals. The judiciary exists to safeguard personal liberty, not to impose the will of the state upon the private lives of its citizens. The courts shall not function as an instrument of social control, nor shall they prioritize the demands of lawmakers over the fundamental rights of individuals to live freely and without interference.

Judicial proceedings shall be conducted with full transparency, ensuring that no case is decided in secrecy, no ruling is issued without justification, and no court functions as an insulated power above public scrutiny. All judicial decisions shall be made accessible to the public, and no legal interpretation shall remain hidden from the people it affects. No system shall exist that allows the courts to operate without oversight, and any attempt to shield judicial proceedings from the public shall be treated as an act of corruption. The judiciary is not an institution that operates in isolation, but a fundamental component of democracy, and no court shall be permitted to function beyond the reach of the people it serves.

No judge shall be permitted to engage in financial conflicts of interest, accept gifts from private entities, or leverage their position for personal gain. The judiciary must remain independent from corporate influence, and no legal ruling shall be issued that serves the financial interests of private institutions at the expense of public welfare. Judges shall not accept appointments to corporate boards, engage in undisclosed financial dealings, or rule on cases in which they have personal investments or affiliations. Any judge found engaging in corruption, financial self-dealing, or decisions influenced by private gain shall be immediately removed from the bench and prosecuted under the full weight of the law. The courts shall not be an extension of corporate power, nor shall they function as a shield for those who seek to use the law to reinforce economic inequality.

The courts shall prioritize the protection of the vulnerable over the preservation of existing power structures. No ruling shall be issued that disproportionately harms the poor, the marginalized, or those without the financial means to defend themselves. The legal system shall not favor those with wealth over those without, and no system shall exist that allows individuals to evade justice through financial advantage. The right to legal representation shall be absolute, ensuring that no person faces trial, sentencing, or legal proceedings without access to adequate defense. The function of the judiciary shall be to serve justice, not to protect the interests of the elite, and no decision shall be issued that undermines the fundamental principle that all people are equal under the law.

No ruling shall be issued that criminalizes poverty, and no judicial decision shall be permitted to disproportionately punish those already burdened by economic inequality. The courts shall not serve as instruments of punitive control, and no legal framework shall exist that prioritizes incarceration, financial penalties, or excessive sentencing over the repair and restoration of justice. The judiciary shall function as a system of fairness, ensuring that no individual is punished more harshly due to their economic status, race, or background. Sentencing laws shall be reformed to remove the structural biases that have long perpetuated cycles of systemic oppression, and any judicial ruling that reinforces discrimination, economic disparity, or social injustice shall be deemed unconstitutional.

The judiciary shall be accountable to the people, ensuring that no court operates as an unchecked force beyond the reach of the nation it serves. No judge shall hold their position indefinitely, no court shall issue rulings that function as instruments of control, and no law shall be interpreted in a manner that prioritizes power over people. The judiciary exists not to dictate the course of justice but to ensure that justice remains an accessible, transparent, and fair process for all. The courts shall not be a system of control, but a mechanism of protection, ensuring that no person, institution, or government body is beyond the reach of the people or above the law.

The judiciary shall remain independent from the influence of the legislative and executive branches, ensuring that no court functions as a political tool or an extension of partisan governance. No President, legislator, or government official shall have the authority to pressure, interfere with, or dictate the rulings of any judicial body. The courts shall not operate in deference to political leaders, nor shall any judge rule in favor of government interests over the constitutional rights of individuals. The judiciary must act as a check on power, not a collaborator in its consolidation. Any attempt by an elected official to influence judicial rulings, install justices for political gain, or undermine the independence of the courts shall be treated as an act of corruption, subject to legal consequences and immediate removal from office.

The judicial system shall be structured to guarantee equal access to justice for all individuals, regardless of economic status, identity, or social standing. No person shall be denied legal representation due to their inability to pay, and no ruling shall be issued that disproportionately harms those without financial means. Public legal defense services shall be fully funded, ensuring that every person receives fair representation in the courts. The right to a fair trial shall not be conditional upon wealth, and no system shall exist that allows individuals to evade justice through financial privilege. Bail, pretrial detention, and other punitive measures that disproportionately target the poor shall be abolished, ensuring that no person is jailed simply for lacking financial resources. The legal system shall not be weaponized against the vulnerable, nor shall it function as an enforcer of economic inequality.

No corporation, business entity, or private interest shall possess the ability to manipulate, influence, or shape judicial rulings to serve its financial agenda. The courts shall not function as an ally to corporate power, and no ruling shall be issued that prioritizes profit over people. Any law or legal precedent that allows corporations to evade liability, exploit labor, or control essential public resources shall be deemed unconstitutional. The judiciary shall uphold the fundamental principle that human rights outweigh corporate interests, and no company shall be permitted to use the courts to suppress workers, evade environmental responsibility, or avoid legal accountability. Judges found engaging in corporate favoritism, accepting financial incentives, or ruling in favor of private interests over public well-being shall face immediate removal and criminal prosecution.

The function of the judiciary is to protect and expand civil rights, not to restrict them. No ruling shall be issued that diminishes the freedoms of marginalized communities, and no law shall be upheld that violates the rights of any individual based on race, gender, sexual orientation, disability, or economic status. The courts shall not function as a gatekeeper of oppression, nor shall any judicial body possess the authority to justify discrimination under the pretense of legal interpretation. The right to marry, to receive medical care, to express identity, and to exist without persecution shall be absolute, and no ruling shall be issued that erodes these freedoms. Any court that seeks to diminish the civil liberties of individuals shall be recognized as acting in violation of the Constitution, and any judge who upholds laws that restrict fundamental rights shall be subject to immediate removal.

The judiciary shall uphold the fundamental right to bodily autonomy, ensuring that no law is permitted that forces medical decisions upon individuals without their consent. No government, court, or institution shall possess the authority to control reproductive healthcare, to deny access to gender-affirming medical treatment, or to impose restrictions on medical procedures that are necessary for the well-being of the individual. Any law that interferes with a person's right to make private medical decisions shall be deemed unconstitutional, and no ruling shall be issued that grants the state control over the bodies of its people. The courts shall not function as enforcers of religious dogma, nor shall any judge be permitted to rule in favor of policies that impose faith-based medical restrictions upon those who do not share those beliefs. The law shall recognize bodily autonomy as a fundamental right, and any ruling that seeks to strip individuals of control over their own healthcare shall be null and void.

The courts shall ensure that the criminal justice system functions as a mechanism for rehabilitation and restoration, rather than a tool of control and punishment. Sentencing laws shall be structured to focus on repairing harm, not enacting vengeance, and no individual shall be subject to excessive or inhumane penalties. The death penalty shall be abolished, as no government shall possess the authority to determine who lives and who dies. The prison system shall not function as a for-profit industry, and no individual shall be incarcerated for the purpose of economic exploitation. No judge shall impose sentences that serve to sustain the private prison industry, nor shall any ruling be issued that incentivizes incarceration as a means of maintaining a labor force. Any laws that disproportionately criminalize specific communities shall be invalidated, and any judge found issuing sentences based on racial bias or economic discrimination shall face immediate removal.

The judiciary shall not be immune from scrutiny, and mechanisms for public accountability shall ensure that no judge is beyond reproach. No ruling shall be unchallengeable, and no decision shall be beyond review. The people shall retain the right to call for the removal of judges who engage in corruption, bias, or misconduct, ensuring that the courts remain an institution of justice rather than a hierarchy of power. No branch of government, including the judiciary, shall be permitted to shield itself from the people, and any judge who fails in their duty to uphold the principles of fairness, equality, and justice shall be held accountable. The courts shall not serve as a closed system operating in secrecy, but as an open and transparent institution, bound to the will and oversight of the public.

The judiciary exists as a guardian of justice, not as a fortress of control. No law shall be upheld that diminishes the dignity of the people, and no ruling shall be issued that prioritizes power over rights. The courts shall function as a means of protecting democracy, ensuring that the government remains one that serves the people, not one that governs them through force, coercion, or legal manipulation. The Constitution guarantees the right to justice for all, and the judiciary shall remain a system that enforces this principle, ensuring that no person, no institution, and no government is above the law.

Article IV: The Right to a Future

Citizenship is not merely a matter of legal status or national affiliation, it is a guarantee of access to the basic conditions necessary for a dignified life. A government that recognizes its legitimacy as derived from the people must not merely acknowledge the existence of its citizens but ensure their ability to live freely, securely, and without undue hardship. The function of the state is not to serve as a passive observer while wealth determines who thrives and who suffers, nor is it to act as a broker auctioning off the resources essential to human survival to the highest bidder. No nation can call itself just if it permits corporations, private interests, or economic forces to dictate access to healthcare, education, or the natural environment upon which all life depends. The people of this nation are not commodities, nor are they expendable in the pursuit of financial profit, and under no circumstances shall the government allow essential rights to be determined by the ability to pay. The right to a future is not a privilege, it is an unalienable guarantee, and any law, policy, or system that undermines this right shall be abolished.

The right to healthcare shall be absolute, ensuring that no person is denied medical treatment due to economic status, employment, or geographic location. No private entity shall have the authority to determine whether an individual receives care, nor shall profit be a factor in decisions regarding life, death, or well-being. The healthcare system shall not be a marketplace, and no insurance company, pharmaceutical corporation, or hospital network shall be permitted to exploit the needs of the sick for financial gain. All medical services shall be provided as a public good, free from the constraints of financial barriers, and no citizen shall be forced into poverty, debt, or bankruptcy due to illness or injury. The government shall ensure that all people have access to comprehensive medical care, including preventive treatment, emergency services, mental health support, and reproductive healthcare. No law shall restrict access to necessary medical procedures, and no political or religious ideology shall dictate the availability of treatment. Healthcare is not a product to be sold, nor a privilege to be earned, it is a fundamental right, and the government shall not permit it to be controlled by those who seek to profit from human suffering.

Education shall be recognized as a public right, ensuring that all individuals have access to knowledge, skill development, and intellectual growth without financial restriction. No person shall be denied an education due to their ability to pay, and no institution of learning shall operate as a business that extracts wealth from those seeking to better themselves. Public education, from early childhood through higher learning, shall be fully funded, ensuring that no student is forced into debt in exchange for access to knowledge. No person shall be trapped in cycles of poverty due to the burden of tuition costs, and no financial institution shall be permitted to exploit students through predatory lending. The pursuit of education shall be free from corporate control, and no private entity shall have the authority to dictate curricula, set policies, or determine the direction of public instruction. Schools shall serve as institutions of learning, not as mechanisms for producing a compliant workforce to serve the interests of capital. The right to education is a guarantee of opportunity, and the government shall ensure that every individual, regardless of background, has access to the tools they need to thrive.

A livable environment is an inalienable right, ensuring that no individual is forced to endure conditions that threaten their survival, health, or ability to sustain life. The air, water, and land of this nation do not belong to corporations, nor are they assets to be traded, exploited, or destroyed in the pursuit of short-term profit. No private entity shall have the authority to poison the water supply, pollute the atmosphere, or strip the land of its ability to sustain life. Environmental degradation is an act of violence against the people, and any industry, government official, or corporate body that engages in the destruction of natural resources for financial gain shall be held accountable. No law shall be passed that allows for the privatization of essential environmental resources, and no corporation shall be permitted to extract, refine, or sell what rightfully belongs to all. The preservation of the planet is not a secondary concern, it is a foundational necessity for the existence of future generations, and the government shall recognize that its duty extends beyond immediate political cycles to the long-term well-being of all inhabitants of this nation and the world.

The government shall not abandon its people to the whims of the market, nor shall it allow wealth to determine who may live securely and who must struggle for survival. No economic system that permits mass homelessness, hunger, or preventable illness shall be considered legitimate, and no policy shall be maintained that prioritizes financial growth over human welfare. The right to a future is not merely about ensuring that individuals survive, it is about ensuring that they may live with dignity, security, and the ability to pursue their aspirations without the constant threat of deprivation. The people shall not be forced to compete for access to basic needs, and no government that allows wealth to dictate survival shall be tolerated. The duty of governance is to protect, uplift, and ensure that every person has the foundation necessary to build a meaningful life. No law, system, or structure that undermines this duty shall be permitted to stand.

The right to a future is not limited to the provision of healthcare, education, and environmental preservation, it extends to the fundamental guarantee that every person shall have the material security necessary to live without fear of destitution, displacement, or exploitation. No government that allows its people to live without stable housing, food, or economic security can claim to serve justice. The availability of shelter, nutrition, and financial stability shall not be dictated by the whims of the market, nor shall these necessities be controlled by those who seek to profit from artificial scarcity. No person shall be left homeless while properties sit vacant for speculation, no child shall go hungry while corporations hoard food supplies to manipulate prices, and no worker shall be denied the ability to sustain themselves while wealth accumulates in the hands of the few. The basic needs of life shall not be conditional upon the accumulation of capital, and no government that permits deprivation to persist shall be considered legitimate in the eyes of justice.

Housing shall be recognized as a right, not as a privilege determined by economic standing. No individual shall be denied access to shelter, nor shall any person be subjected to forced displacement due to financial hardship. No corporation, landlord, or financial institution shall be permitted to hoard housing stock, manipulate rent prices, or extract wealth from those who are simply seeking to live. The government shall ensure that all individuals have access to safe, affordable housing, free from predatory lending, price inflation, or market speculation that treats shelter as an investment rather than a necessity. No law shall be passed that allows for mass evictions, and no person shall be criminalized for living in poverty. Housing shall be provided as a public service, ensuring that no one is forced into homelessness due to circumstances beyond their control. The function of governance is to protect its people, and no nation that allows its citizens to be discarded into the streets shall be considered just.

The right to food security shall be absolute, ensuring that no person is forced to suffer from hunger while food supplies are wasted, destroyed, or hoarded for financial gain. No corporation shall have the authority to manipulate food production, withhold essential nutrition, or create artificial shortages for profit. Agriculture shall serve the people, not the market, and no system shall exist that prioritizes export profits over domestic food stability. Farmers shall be protected from exploitation by corporate agribusiness, ensuring that land remains in the hands of those who cultivate it rather than those who seek to monopolize it. No community shall be subjected to food deserts, and no individual shall go without nourishment due to financial constraints. Food is not a luxury, it is a necessity, and no person shall be forced to beg, compete, or suffer in its pursuit. The government shall ensure that all individuals have access to adequate nutrition, free from the distortions of price speculation, industrial waste, or supply manipulation by those who see hunger as an opportunity for profit.

The right to economic stability shall be protected, ensuring that no person is left to suffer due to the volatility of financial markets, the failures of industry, or the systemic exploitation of labor. No worker shall be subjected to conditions that deny them the ability to sustain a dignified life, and no employer shall be permitted to extract wealth from labor while providing wages that do not meet the basic cost of survival. The right to fair compensation shall be guaranteed, ensuring that no person is forced to work multiple jobs, endure exploitative contracts, or sacrifice their health and well-being simply to afford the necessities of life. The government shall implement policies that protect workers from predatory employment practices, ensuring that no industry, corporation, or employer is permitted to treat human labor as a disposable commodity. Universal basic income, wage protections, and labor rights shall be established to guarantee that all individuals have the financial security necessary to participate fully in society without being subjected to conditions of servitude. No person shall be abandoned to poverty, and no system shall exist that forces individuals to suffer in order to sustain the profits of the wealthy.

The right to a future extends beyond survival, it guarantees that individuals shall have the ability to build, dream, and pursue a life of fulfillment without the constant threat of instability. No government that restricts opportunity, stifles potential, or enforces generational cycles of deprivation can claim to serve its people. The role of governance is not merely to provide the bare minimum for existence, but to create the conditions in which all individuals may thrive, contribute, and participate in the shaping of a just and equitable society. This Constitution does not recognize suffering as an inevitability, nor does it accept deprivation as an unfortunate reality, it mandates that the government shall act as a force against all systems that perpetuate inequality, ensuring that no person is denied the right to a future simply because they were born into a world that has long prioritized profit over people. The right to live with dignity, security, and opportunity is not a theoretical ideal, it is a non-negotiable demand, and any institution, policy, or law that undermines this right shall be abolished.

Article V: Amendments Must Expand Rights, Not Restrict
Them

The purpose of constitutional amendments is to refine,
strengthen, and expand the principles of justice, ensuring
that the foundation of governance remains responsive to the
evolving needs of the people. Amendments shall exist as
instruments of progress, never as mechanisms of regression.
No amendment shall be enacted that restricts fundamental
rights, undermines democratic governance, or reverses the
protections guaranteed by this Constitution. The function of
an amendment is not to erode liberty but to reinforce it, and
any attempt to alter the Constitution in a manner that
reduces the rights of individuals, grants undue power to the
state, or imposes artificial limitations on personal autonomy
shall be deemed unconstitutional. The government shall not
permit the will of the people to be manipulated through
legislative or judicial processes designed to roll back progress.
Any law, ruling, or amendment that seeks to strip individuals
of their freedoms shall be recognized as a violation of the
fundamental principles upon which this nation stands and
shall be rendered null and void.

No amendment shall be passed that restricts or revokes the
right to vote, the right to personal autonomy, the right to fair
representation, or any other right enshrined within this
Constitution. The expansion of rights shall be the only
acceptable use of the amendment process, and under no
circumstances shall any government, legislative body, or
judicial authority have the power to reduce the scope of
freedom that has already been secured. Any proposed

amendment that seeks to disenfranchise, exclude, or diminish the rights of any group shall be rejected outright, and any law that attempts to circumvent constitutional protections in order to impose restrictions on individual liberty shall be struck down. The government shall not have the authority to redefine human rights in a way that limits them, nor shall it possess the ability to determine that certain rights may be selectively revoked based on changing political priorities, economic interests, or social pressures. The rights of the people are not conditional, they are absolute, and no amendment that threatens them shall be permitted.

The process of amending the Constitution shall remain open, transparent, and subject to the will of the people, not to the maneuverings of those in power. No amendment shall be passed without the direct and informed consent of the public, and no amendment shall be enacted through legislative manipulation, partisan advantage, or judicial fiat. The people must retain control over the process of constitutional change, ensuring that amendments serve their interests rather than the interests of those who seek to control them. No amendment shall be proposed or ratified without a full national vote, and no system shall exist that allows amendments to be passed through legislative channels that bypass the direct participation of the people. A government that allows the Constitution to be altered without the full consent of those it serves is not a democracy, and no law shall be maintained that permits such a distortion of the amendment process.

Amendments that seek to guarantee additional rights, protections, and freedoms shall be prioritized, ensuring that the Constitution remains a living document that grows in accordance with the needs of its people. The expansion of civil rights, labor protections, environmental justice, and economic security shall be treated as legitimate purposes for constitutional amendments, while any attempt to restrict or repeal existing protections shall be immediately disqualified.

The purpose of governance is to secure the well-being of its people, and any amendment that seeks to narrow the scope of justice, to impose new forms of control, or to limit access to fundamental rights shall be rejected outright. This Constitution shall not be weaponized against those it is meant to serve, and no law shall be passed that grants the government the authority to dismantle the protections that ensure human dignity and freedom.

The repeal of unjust amendments shall be a recognized and protected function of the Constitution, ensuring that any amendment passed in error, through coercion, or as a means of subjugation may be overturned. The Constitution shall not be a rigid document that upholds the mistakes of the past, nor shall it serve as a barrier to correcting historical injustices. Any amendment that has failed to uphold the principles of liberty and justice, that has served as a mechanism of discrimination, or that has allowed the suppression of rights shall be removed from the constitutional framework. No government shall be required to maintain laws that contradict the core values of equality, fairness, and democratic governance, and no amendment shall be preserved if it serves as an obstacle to the pursuit of justice. The ability to repeal harmful amendments shall be as essential as the ability to introduce new protections, ensuring that the Constitution remains a force for progress rather than a tool for oppression.

The existence of this Constitution is to serve the people, not to function as an unchangeable doctrine that resists necessary reform. Amendments shall be utilized to ensure that governance remains just, equitable, and adaptable to the needs of the nation, not as a means of preserving outdated systems, ideologies, or policies that no longer serve the interests of the people. The process of amending the Constitution shall remain an act of collective will, shaped by the voices of those it governs, ensuring that no single generation dictates the future for all who come after. No amendment shall be treated as sacrosanct if it has failed in its purpose, and no amendment shall be beyond the reach of change if the people demand its correction. The Constitution exists as a living document, one that evolves in service of those it protects, and the process of amendment shall reflect this truth.

The process of amending the Constitution shall remain under the exclusive authority of the people, ensuring that no government, political party, or corporate entity may manipulate or obstruct the expansion of justice. No amendment shall be proposed, debated, or enacted in secrecy, and no law shall be passed that limits public participation in the process of constitutional change. Amendments shall require a national referendum, with full access to public debate, analysis, and discussion, ensuring that all citizens are informed participants in the evolution of their own governance. The Constitution shall not be altered through legislative deals, judicial maneuvering, or executive power, it is a contract between the people and their government, and any change to its structure must be made with their direct and overwhelming consent. No amendment shall be introduced that benefits the ruling class at the expense of the majority, and any attempt to manipulate the amendment process to serve private interests shall be recognized as an act of constitutional corruption, subject to legal action and immediate nullification.

The power of amendment shall never be used to enshrine privilege, expand systemic inequality, or reinforce structures of control that serve the few at the expense of the many. No amendment shall be passed that restricts voting rights, entrenches economic hierarchy, or codifies legal advantages for any group based on wealth, status, or political affiliation. The Constitution is not a tool for the protection of elite power, and any amendment that seeks to secure control for those already in positions of influence shall be rejected outright. The amendment process must serve the expansion of democracy, ensuring that governance remains accessible, accountable, and subject to continuous refinement in favor of the people. Under no circumstances shall an amendment be permitted that entrenches corporate influence over public policy, grants legal immunity to those in power, or diminishes the ability of the people to challenge their own government. Any amendment that shields institutions, corporations, or individuals from accountability shall be deemed unconstitutional, as no system can claim legitimacy if it places power beyond the reach of those it governs.

No amendment shall restrict bodily autonomy, limit access to healthcare, or impose artificial constraints upon the rights of individuals to make private medical decisions. The Constitution shall not be altered in ways that allow the government to interfere with reproductive healthcare, gender-affirming medical treatment, or the right of individuals to refuse medical procedures. No law shall be upheld that forces individuals to carry pregnancies against their will, to undergo medical interventions without consent, or to submit to restrictions on their physical autonomy for the sake of political or religious agendas. The Constitution exists to guarantee freedom, not to justify oppression, and any amendment that attempts to redefine autonomy as a conditional right shall be struck down. The government shall not possess the authority to legislate control over the human body, and no legal framework shall exist that allows fundamental healthcare decisions to be dictated by the state.

Amendments that reinforce environmental protections, labor rights, and economic justice shall be prioritized, ensuring that the Constitution serves not only present generations but those who will inherit the consequences of today's governance. No amendment shall be passed that permits the continued destruction of the planet, the unchecked exploitation of workers, or the consolidation of wealth in the hands of the few. The amendment process shall be a tool for securing long-term sustainability, ensuring that economic systems remain fair, resources remain available for future generations, and no industry, corporation, or government policy is allowed to strip the earth of its ability to sustain life. No amendment shall be ratified that allows for corporate ownership of essential resources, and no law shall exist that enables private entities to profit from the depletion of public goods. The rights of future generations must be protected with the same force as the rights of those living today, and any amendment that fails to consider the long-term consequences of governance shall be deemed illegitimate.

The repeal of unjust amendments shall be recognized as an essential function of the Constitution, ensuring that laws and policies that have served as instruments of oppression are not allowed to persist indefinitely. Any amendment that has been used to justify discrimination, economic exploitation, or political control shall be subject to review and removal, ensuring that the mistakes of the past do not remain enshrined in the legal framework of the present. The Constitution shall not be treated as a document that preserves injustice under the pretense of historical continuity, it shall be a living framework that prioritizes correction, adaptation, and the expansion of justice over the maintenance of outdated or harmful policies. The right to challenge and repeal harmful amendments shall be protected, ensuring that no law is above revision, no ruling is beyond reconsideration, and no amendment shall remain in place if it has failed to serve the fundamental principles of equality, fairness, and human dignity.

The Constitution exists to serve the people, not to limit them. No government shall possess the authority to use the amendment process as a means of control, and no law shall be passed that obstructs the people's ability to shape their own governance. The expansion of rights shall always be prioritized over their restriction, and the function of amendments shall be to ensure that progress is not undone by those who fear change. The Constitution shall remain a force for liberation, not a tool of restriction, and any attempt to alter its foundation in ways that diminish justice shall be met with the full resistance of the people it was written to protect.

Article VI: The Separation of Church and State is Absolute

The government shall not establish, fund, endorse, or legislate based on religious belief. The separation of church and state is not a suggestion, an ideal, or a negotiable principle, it is a fundamental requirement of a just and free society. No democracy can function when its laws are dictated by theological interpretations, nor can governance remain fair when religious institutions are granted influence over policy, public funds, or the rights of individuals. Religion, in all its forms, is a private and personal matter, not the foundation of law, and under no circumstances shall any government body, elected official, or judicial authority use religious doctrine as a basis for governance. The law must serve all people equally, without regard to faith, ensuring that no group is privileged above another based on religious identity, and that no citizen is forced to live under laws derived from a belief system they do not share.

No religious institution shall receive public funding, tax exemptions, or financial benefits from the government. The state shall not subsidize churches, religious schools, faith-based charities, or any organization that operates under the authority of religious doctrine. Public money shall not be used to support religious education, maintain places of worship, or fund programs that require participation in faith-based practices. Religious institutions, like all other private organizations, shall be subject to taxation, ensuring that no faith group is granted financial privilege at the expense of the public. No law shall exempt religious organizations from financial responsibility, and no religious institution shall be permitted to operate as a tax-free entity while engaging in political lobbying, discrimination, or efforts to influence legislation. The government shall not provide grants, property, or financial incentives to religious groups, nor shall it allow any faith-based institution to dictate the allocation of public resources. The neutrality of the state in matters of faith must be absolute, ensuring that no citizen is compelled to fund, support, or abide by religious practices through their tax dollars or public institutions.

No law shall be passed that imposes religious doctrine on the public, whether directly or indirectly. The legal system shall not recognize religious objections as a basis for restricting the rights of others, nor shall the government pass legislation that enforces religious morality on those who do not subscribe to it. The courts shall not rule in favor of faith-based exemptions that violate civil rights, and no individual or institution shall be permitted to refuse services, employment, or medical care based on religious belief. The government shall not interfere with private faith, nor shall it suppress religious expression, but it shall not allow religious organizations, institutions, or individuals to impose their beliefs upon others through law, policy, or institutional control.

Religious practices shall remain separate from public governance in all forms. No official oath of office shall require a religious affirmation, nor shall any government proceeding include mandatory prayer, religious readings, or ceremonies invoking divine authority. No legislative body shall begin its sessions with religious rituals, no government institution shall display religious symbols, and no court shall use religious texts as a basis for legal decisions. Public schools shall not include religious instruction in their curricula, nor shall they be required to observe religious holidays or accommodate faith-based teachings in any form. The neutrality of the state is essential in ensuring that public spaces, institutions, and policies remain free from religious favoritism, allowing all citizens to participate fully in society without coercion or exclusion.

No individual shall be forced to adhere to the religious beliefs of others in medical, legal, or civil matters. The government shall not allow religious institutions to dictate medical policies, restrict access to reproductive healthcare, or interfere with end-of-life decisions. No hospital, clinic, or medical provider shall be permitted to deny care based on religious objections, and no law shall be passed that limits medical access due to faith-based reasoning. Bodily autonomy is a fundamental right, and no government shall enforce laws that compel individuals to conform to religious doctrine regarding birth control, abortion, gender-affirming care, or other private medical decisions. The right to medical treatment shall not be subject to the beliefs of those in positions of authority, and no patient shall be denied necessary care due to the religious convictions of a provider, employer, or governing body.

Religious organizations shall not be permitted to operate outside the bounds of civil law, nor shall faith-based groups receive special legal protections that allow them to discriminate, exploit, or evade accountability. No religious leader, institution, or organization shall be exempt from the laws that govern the public, and no faith-based institution shall be granted immunity from prosecution for crimes committed under the guise of religious practice. Religious groups that engage in fraud, abuse, financial misconduct, or any form of criminal activity shall be subject to full legal prosecution, with no exceptions granted based on religious status. The courts shall not recognize religious belief as a defense for harm, nor shall faith be invoked to justify child marriage, conversion therapy, abuse, labor exploitation, or any other act that violates human rights. The government shall not recognize religious arbitration in place of civil law, ensuring that all citizens have equal access to legal protection, regardless of their affiliation with a religious institution.

Religious exemptions shall not extend to laws protecting civil rights, ensuring that no faith-based organization, employer, or individual is permitted to discriminate against others under the pretense of religious conscience. No business shall refuse service based on religious objections to gender identity, sexual orientation, race, or marital status, and no faith-based institution shall be allowed to circumvent anti-discrimination laws in hiring, housing, education, or public services. The government shall not grant religious organizations the ability to deny rights to those who do not conform to their beliefs, nor shall faith be used as a means to justify exclusion, prejudice, or segregation. The right to worship freely does not include the right to infringe upon the freedoms of others, and under no circumstances shall religious liberty be interpreted as a license to deny legal equality.

The separation of church and state is the foundation of a democratic society, ensuring that no government is controlled by religious authority and no law is written to serve the interests of faith over the rights of the people. The government shall remain secular in all matters, governing by reason, evidence, and the collective will of the people rather than theological doctrine. The law serves all citizens equally, regardless of their personal beliefs, and no system shall exist that forces adherence to religious principles upon those who do not accept them. Faith is a personal choice, and it shall remain a private matter, wholly distinct from the function of governance. No nation that allows religious rule can claim to be a democracy, and no law that enforces faith can be considered just. The government shall govern, religion shall remain personal, and the rights of all shall be upheld, free from the control, influence, or imposition of religious ideology.

Article VII: The Purpose of Law is Protection, Not Power

The purpose of law is to protect, not to control. The government exists to serve the people, not to govern through coercion, force, or fear. No law shall be written, passed, or upheld that functions as an instrument of oppression rather than a tool of justice. No policy shall be enacted that prioritizes the maintenance of power over the well-being of those it claims to serve. The legal system shall not be a mechanism for the domination of the many by the few, nor shall it be used to shield those in power from accountability while punishing those without wealth, influence, or protection. The law must function as a safeguard against injustice, not as an enforcer of hierarchy. No institution shall possess the authority to impose laws that restrict the rights of individuals in the name of order, nor shall any law be upheld that serves only to reinforce economic disparity, racial injustice, or systemic control over marginalized communities. The role of governance is to protect the dignity, autonomy, and safety of all people, ensuring that justice is accessible, impartial, and immune to corruption.

No law shall exist that disproportionately punishes the poor while shielding the wealthy from consequence. The legal system shall not function as a debtor's prison, a tool for the protection of corporate interests, or a means of punishing those who lack financial security. No person shall be incarcerated for poverty, nor shall the legal code include penalties that exist solely to extract wealth from those who have none to give. Fines, bail requirements, and legal fees shall be structured to ensure that no person is imprisoned, indebted, or permanently disadvantaged due to their inability to pay. No individual shall be subjected to harsher sentencing, prolonged imprisonment, or permanent disenfranchisement based on their economic status, race, or social standing. The right to due process shall be absolute, ensuring that no one is denied legal representation, fair trial proceedings, or access to appeal. The courts shall not favor those with the means to afford private defense while leaving those without resources to navigate a system designed to entrap them. No law shall be crafted with the intention of disproportionately harming the poor while allowing the rich to evade justice.

The rights of women, the poor, and the marginalized shall be protected first, not last. No law shall exist that subordinates women, diminishes their autonomy, or dictates the terms of their existence based on outdated moral, religious, or patriarchal constructs. The legal system shall not function as an enforcer of gender oppression, nor shall it be structured to restrict the freedoms of women under the guise of protection. Bodily autonomy shall be absolute, ensuring that no government, religious institution, or judicial ruling has the authority to control reproductive healthcare, access to contraception, or decisions regarding pregnancy. No law shall be passed that forces women into economic dependence, denies them access to financial independence, or restricts their ability to participate fully in society. Women shall not be penalized for seeking divorce, for choosing to remain unmarried, or for pursuing lives outside the traditional expectations imposed upon them by outdated laws. No system shall exist that treats women as property, as legal extensions of their husbands, or as second-class citizens under the law.

Laws shall be written to serve those most vulnerable to harm, not those most insulated from it. No legal system that functions primarily to protect corporations, the wealthy, and the powerful can be considered just, and any legal framework that prioritizes economic interests over human dignity shall be dismantled. The role of the law is not to protect the profits of businesses while leaving workers without rights, nor is it to ensure the financial success of industries while allowing consumers to be exploited, underpaid, or left without recourse. No legal loophole shall exist that permits corporations to evade labor protections, to circumvent safety regulations, or to operate without accountability for the harm they cause. No law shall exist that grants businesses the power to extract wealth from workers while denying them fair wages, benefits, or protections against abuse. The government shall not function as an enforcer of corporate interests at the expense of the people, and any law that enables systemic exploitation shall be repealed.

The legal system shall prioritize repair, not domination. Punitive justice systems that exist solely to incarcerate, criminalize, and punish shall be reformed, ensuring that the law functions as a means of rehabilitation rather than an instrument of control. No government shall enact policies that prioritize the expansion of prisons over the expansion of opportunity, nor shall any law be passed that focuses solely on punishment while failing to address the root causes of crime. The criminal justice system shall not serve as an industry, and no law shall exist that allows for the privatization of incarceration, the profit-driven expansion of prison facilities, or the use of prison labor as a means of corporate enrichment. The government shall not permit mass incarceration as a substitute for economic, educational, and social investment. No individual shall be sentenced to a life of poverty, disenfranchisement, or permanent criminal status for offenses that do not pose harm to society, and no law shall function as a tool for the mass imprisonment of specific communities, particularly communities of color, the impoverished, and the politically disenfranchised.

The law exists to uphold justice, not to maintain an illusion of order built on the suppression of certain groups. No legal system shall be structured in a way that justifies racial disparities in policing, sentencing, or incarceration rates, and any law that has historically been used to criminalize marginalized communities shall be repealed. The government shall not permit the use of excessive force, racial profiling, or discriminatory legal practices, ensuring that no law enforcement agency, court, or judge is permitted to operate in a way that disproportionately harms people of color, immigrants, or those deemed undesirable by those in power. No law shall exist that grants law enforcement agencies the ability to act with impunity, nor shall any system be maintained that allows police officers to evade accountability for acts of violence, corruption, or abuse. The people shall not be subjected to surveillance, intimidation, or unchecked policing, and any law that grants the state excessive authority to monitor, detain, or criminalize its citizens shall be deemed unconstitutional.

The law shall not exist to serve the ruling class, to protect wealth over humanity, or to reinforce systems of oppression under the guise of maintaining order. No policy shall be passed that disproportionately harms the most vulnerable while granting privilege to those who already hold power. The purpose of governance is not to control the people, but to serve them, ensuring that all laws function as mechanisms of fairness, security, and equal protection. Any law that contradicts this fundamental principle shall not be permitted to stand.

The law shall not be wielded as a weapon of control, nor shall it function as a means of maintaining systemic inequality. No government that claims to serve the people shall permit the continued existence of legal frameworks designed to suppress political dissent, silence opposition, or restrict the rights of those who challenge the status quo. No law shall be passed that criminalizes protest, assembly, or the ability of the people to organize against injustice. The right to oppose, to speak, to demand change shall be absolute, and any attempt to restrict these freedoms under the pretense of security, order, or public interest shall be deemed unconstitutional. No government shall have the authority to label opposition as criminal behavior, nor shall law enforcement agencies be permitted to use their power to suppress movements for justice. The people shall not be policed into submission, nor shall the state deploy surveillance, infiltration, or harassment as a means of controlling political activism. No law shall exist that grants the state the ability to suppress democratic engagement, and no ruling shall be issued that enables the criminalization of those who fight for the expansion of rights.

The legal system shall be accessible to all, ensuring that justice is not reserved for those with the financial resources to secure representation, challenge injustice, or manipulate the courts to their advantage. No person shall be denied legal recourse due to their inability to afford legal fees, and no government shall maintain a judicial system that functions primarily to serve those with the means to navigate its complexities. Public legal defense services shall be fully funded, ensuring that no individual is left to defend themselves against a system designed to favor those in positions of power. The courts shall not be places of privilege where wealth determines outcomes, and no corporation, politician, or private entity shall be granted legal protections unavailable to the public. The principle of equal justice under the law shall not be rhetorical, it shall be an absolute requirement of governance, ensuring that no system exists that allows those with financial means to evade accountability while those without resources suffer the full weight of legal consequences.

The function of law enforcement shall be to protect, not to punish. No police force shall be structured as an occupying power within communities, nor shall any law exist that permits law enforcement agencies to operate without oversight, accountability, or direct public scrutiny. No officer of the law shall be immune from prosecution for acts of brutality, corruption, or misconduct, and no government shall maintain systems that allow for the continued abuse of police power. No law shall protect law enforcement agencies from investigation, nor shall legal immunity be granted to those who violate the rights of the people under the pretense of maintaining order. The use of force shall not be the first response to crisis, and no government shall authorize lethal violence as a standard policing tactic. The function of law enforcement shall not be to intimidate, detain, or control, it shall be to ensure the safety of all, with measures in place to prevent the abuse of authority and the unchecked militarization of policing. No agency shall be permitted to deploy surveillance technology, conduct mass arrests, or enforce laws that disproportionately target communities of color, immigrants, or political dissidents. The government shall not permit the existence of secret policing agencies, nor shall it allow for the continued use of unconstitutional practices such as indefinite detention, warrantless surveillance, or the targeting of individuals based on race, religion, or political belief.

No law shall be written that expands the power of the government beyond the limits necessary for the protection of its people. No institution shall have the authority to pass laws that favor the interests of the state over the rights of individuals, nor shall any legal precedent be maintained that allows for the indefinite expansion of governmental authority under the pretense of national security. The rights of the people shall not be conditional, subject to restriction in times of crisis or nullified under emergency declarations that serve only to consolidate power in the hands of the few. No law shall be passed that permits the government to suspend constitutional protections, and no legal framework shall exist that allows the state to circumvent due process, violate privacy, or operate beyond the reach of public accountability. The principle of governance by consent shall be absolute, and any law that seeks to erode this foundation shall be repealed.

The rights of the individual shall always outweigh the interests of the state. No law shall be passed that grants the government ownership over the lives, bodies, or freedoms of the people it claims to serve. No policy shall be enacted that imposes forced labor, mandatory service, or any form of government-mandated participation in industries, institutions, or conflicts against the will of the people. The government shall not have the authority to compel service, extract labor, or determine the economic futures of its citizens, ensuring that no law exists that allows individuals to be treated as resources for state interests. No legal framework shall exist that grants the government control over the reproductive choices, medical decisions, or private affairs of its citizens, and no law shall be upheld that permits the government to interfere in matters that belong solely to the individual.

The legal system shall function as a safeguard for justice, not a mechanism for institutional self-preservation. No law shall be written that protects politicians, corporations, or public officials from investigation, prosecution, or removal from office. No legal precedent shall exist that grants lifelong immunity to those in positions of power, nor shall any system be maintained that allows officials to evade consequences through procedural loopholes, political alliances, or financial settlements. The legal process shall apply equally to all, and no individual, regardless of status, shall be placed above the law. The ability of the people to hold their leaders accountable shall be absolute, ensuring that no government is permitted to rule unchecked, and no individual shall remain in power once they have violated the trust of those they serve.

The law exists to protect, not to dominate. No system of governance shall be permitted to sustain itself through oppression, and no legal structure shall remain in place that prioritizes control over justice. The people shall not be ruled through force, deception, or manipulation, and any government that seeks to govern through coercion shall be deemed illegitimate. The role of the state is to ensure the safety, dignity, and well-being of those within its borders, and any law that contradicts this mandate shall be abolished. The law does not exist to serve those in power, it exists to protect those without it.

II.
The Bill of Rights:
Not a Loophole for Tyrants

Part 1: Independence from Oppression, Not Just a King

When first declared, independence was framed as an escape from the tyranny of monarchy, yet it was never extended to all. The first Declaration of Independence did not recognize the enslaved, the dispossessed, the laborers who built the wealth of a nation they would never be permitted to own. It spoke of liberty but preserved bondage, preached equality but upheld a system of power built on subjugation, extraction, and control. It was a document drafted by men who saw themselves as revolutionaries while ensuring that the chains they cast off were simply transferred to others. The freedom they envisioned was not universal, it was exclusive, a privilege meant only for those whose power would remain untouched. This new Declaration does not replicate their omissions, nor does it preserve the hierarchy they sought to maintain. It does not declare independence for some while binding others in servitude. This Declaration recognizes that true freedom is not simply the right to be free from a king, it is the right to be free from oppression in all its forms.

We declare that no government that sustains systems of exploitation shall be considered legitimate, no institution that privileges one class, race, or gender above another shall be recognized as just. Independence shall not be confined to national sovereignty but shall extend to the full liberation of all individuals, ensuring that no system of power is allowed to persist that extracts from the many to enrich the few. No economy that relies on the underpayment, enslavement, or suffering of the working class shall be tolerated. No government that allows corporations to dictate the lives, health, and futures of its people shall be upheld. The right to self-determination is not a rhetorical flourish, nor is it a principle that applies only to those with the financial means to exercise it. True independence is the ability of all people to live without fear of starvation, eviction, lack of medical care, or the inability to access basic necessities. No system that upholds inequality shall be allowed to endure under the pretense of democracy.

We reject the false independence of capitalism, which promises freedom while ensuring dependency on wages that do not sustain, on industries that strip the earth bare, on systems designed to keep the vast majority in cycles of endless labor while a small elite consolidates wealth. We reject the manufactured independence of those who claim that individual success is merely a matter of effort, ignoring the generational structures that ensure wealth remains in the hands of the few while entire communities remain locked out of opportunity. We reject the independence of corporations who claim the right to operate without oversight while their actions destroy the planet, exploit the vulnerable, and purchase the laws that govern them. We reject the independence of billionaires who treat taxes as theft, yet rely on public infrastructure, public land, and public labor to sustain their empires. This Declaration is not one of self-congratulation, not a celebration of a broken system that has allowed a few to thrive while the rest struggle. It is a rejection of the hypocrisy that first defined the so-called independence of this nation.

This Declaration recognizes that a government that governs without justice, without equity, and without care for the people it claims to serve is a government that has forfeited its right to exist. It is not enough to declare independence from a monarch while maintaining rule by oligarchs, from a foreign power while domestic rulers build an empire of inequality. We reject the idea that the preservation of a state

70

is more important than the liberation of its people, that laws written to protect wealth should be preserved even when they deny the basic dignity of those who suffer under them. Independence means nothing if it does not include the right to be free from exploitation, from enforced poverty, from corporate control, from religious imposition, from patriarchal dominance. It means nothing if it does not dismantle the structures that have kept so many in chains, invisible in the grand narrative of a so-called free nation.

The first Declaration spoke of life, liberty, and the pursuit of happiness, yet those rights were written only for men who owned property, who owned people, who saw themselves as the architects of a nation built in their own image. This Declaration reclaims those rights, not as conditional privileges granted by a governing body but as inalienable guarantees owed to every individual. Life is not merely the right to exist but the right to exist with dignity, without the constant threat of economic collapse, environmental destruction, or systemic violence. Liberty is not merely the absence of monarchy but the absence of oppression in all its forms, economic, racial, gendered, religious, and political. The pursuit of happiness is not the pursuit of wealth for the few but the ability of all to live in security, creativity, and community, free from the coercion of systems designed to extract every ounce of labor, time, and energy from those who have no choice but to comply.

We declare independence not only from past tyrannies but from the present ones. From the corporations who claim ownership over the land, water, and air that rightfully belong to all. From the billionaires who believe that their right to wealth supersedes the right of others to survive. From the industries that see people as expendable and the planet as disposable. From the politicians who sell democracy to the highest bidder, who write laws not for the people but for the powerful. From the religious institutions that insist their doctrine should dictate law. From the police who protect property before they protect people, who answer protest with violence, who maintain order through intimidation rather than justice. From the media that serves as the mouthpiece of the wealthy, from the courts that favor those with means, from the systems of education that prepare children not to think but to obey. Independence is meaningless if it does not include the right to dismantle these structures, to refuse compliance with institutions that do not serve the people, to overthrow governments that betray their purpose.

This Declaration does not seek reform, it seeks transformation. It does not ask for the betterment of a broken system but for the construction of a new one. The people have the right to reject any system that fails them, to walk away from laws that do not serve justice, to reclaim power from those who have hoarded it. Independence is not a static achievement but an ongoing act of defiance against those who seek to maintain control. It is a declaration of our right to shape the world we live in, to demand more than survival, to demand more than the illusion of democracy. This is not a Declaration of Independence written by and for a privileged few, it is a declaration of liberation, one that recognizes that freedom has not yet been achieved and that the work of independence is not behind us but ahead.

Part 2: A Government That Serves or Is Dismantled

Governments derive their power from the people, not the other way around. No institution of governance exists by divine right, nor does any government hold power by virtue of tradition, wealth, or inherited authority. A government that does not serve its people has no legitimacy and no claim to continued existence. It is not the people who owe their allegiance to a government, but the government that owes its service to the people. If that service is corrupted, if power is hoarded instead of distributed, if laws are written to protect wealth instead of ensuring justice, if representatives act as rulers rather than as servants, then that government has forfeited the right to govern. The people shall not be bound to a system that works against them. The people shall not be forced into submission under laws that do not protect them. The people shall not be required to sustain a government that has proven itself unworthy of their trust. The legitimacy of any government exists only so long as it upholds the dignity, autonomy, and well-being of those it claims to serve. When it ceases to do so, the people have the right, no, the obligation, to dismantle it and build anew.

A government that serves the people does not enrich itself at their expense. No nation can call itself just while its leaders hoard resources, while wealth flows upward into the hands of the few, while those who govern live in excess while those they govern live in scarcity. The concentration of wealth is the concentration of power, and no government that allows economic disparity to reach extremes shall be permitted to stand. No industry shall be allowed to dictate policy, no corporation shall be permitted to buy legislation, and no billionaire shall be allowed to exist while poverty still remains. The government shall not serve as a shield for the wealthy, protecting their fortunes while denying the people a living wage, universal healthcare, affordable housing, and food security. No system that allows economic survival to depend on endless labor, no law that permits the rich to exploit the labor of the poor, no policy that protects corporate profits over human lives shall be upheld. A government that claims to serve the people must first ensure that every person, regardless of status, has access to the necessities of life without conditions, without debt, and without fear of deprivation. A government that fails to do this is not a government of the people, it is an institution of oppression, and it shall not be allowed to persist.

A government that serves the people does not rule through fear, coercion, or force. No government that enforces obedience through police violence, mass surveillance, imprisonment, or censorship can claim to be democratic. No law shall exist that permits the suppression of protest, the criminalization of dissent, or the silencing of those who speak against injustice. No government shall be permitted to monitor its citizens as if they are criminals, to invade their privacy under the guise of national security, or to strip them of their autonomy under the pretense of maintaining order. No police force shall function as a military, no military shall be turned against its own people, and no agency shall have the power to detain, interrogate, or punish individuals without due process. The rights of the people shall not be suspended in times of crisis, nor shall governments be permitted to invoke emergency powers to justify the expansion of state control. A government that fears its own people is a government that has already failed them, and no institution that relies on force to sustain itself shall be considered legitimate. The right to challenge authority shall not be restricted, and any government that seeks to maintain power by suppressing opposition has already declared itself unfit to govern.

A government that serves the people does not legislate morality, impose religious doctrine, or dictate personal freedoms. The role of governance is to protect, not to control. No law shall exist that dictates what a person may do with their own body, whom they may love, or how they may define themselves. No government shall have the authority to restrict reproductive rights, to deny gender-affirming care, or to impose religious beliefs on those who do not share them. No system of governance shall allow faith to override science, prejudice to dictate policy, or ideology to determine law. The rights of the individual shall be absolute, and any government that seeks to control the private decisions of its people is a government that has abandoned its duty. A government that serves the people does not claim ownership over their bodies, their relationships, or their identities. It ensures their freedom, without restriction, without coercion, and without condition.

A government that serves the people does not recognize itself as infallible. No government shall be permitted to entrench itself beyond the reach of change, to declare itself beyond criticism, or to silence those who demand better. The structures of governance must remain adaptable, ensuring that when laws fail, they can be rewritten; when policies harm, they can be undone; when leaders betray, they can be removed. No system shall be protected for the sake of tradition alone, and no law shall be maintained simply because it has always been. If a law does not serve justice, it is not a law, it is an obstacle to justice, and it must be abolished. No government shall be permitted to prioritize its own preservation over the well-being of its people, and no ruling class shall be allowed to remain in power when it has failed those it was meant to serve.

A government that no longer serves the people shall be dismantled, by any means necessary. If the system cannot be reformed, it must be abandoned. If power cannot be redistributed, it must be taken. If justice cannot be secured within the framework of the existing government, then that government must be replaced with one that recognizes the inherent rights of all individuals. The people are not bound to a government that betrays them, nor are they required to sustain institutions that have proven themselves corrupt. The right to abolish, to overthrow, to create anew is the foundation of true democracy, and no law, constitution, or ruling authority shall deny this fundamental truth.

This is not a declaration of allegiance to a nation, a flag, or a governing body. It is a declaration of allegiance to justice, to freedom, to the principle that governments serve only at the will of the people. When that service is betrayed, when power is hoarded, when laws are written not to protect but to control, the people have the absolute right to reject their government in its entirety. This is not a request for reform, not a plea for policy changes or incremental progress, it is a declaration that no government shall be permitted to exist if it does not serve, protect, and uplift the people. A government that refuses to do so is a government that shall not stand.

III.
The Declaration of Independence: From What, Exactly

Part 1: Independence from Oppression, Not Just a King

No state shall possess the authority to restrict, revoke, or deny fundamental rights that are protected under federal law. The existence of individual states within a national framework does not permit them to function as independent fiefdoms, crafting laws that erode human dignity, deny basic freedoms, or undermine the principles of justice. The idea that certain rights may be recognized in one jurisdiction but denied in another is a failure of governance, a contradiction that has allowed oppression to persist under the guise of state sovereignty. No state shall have the authority to suppress voting rights, deny reproductive healthcare, discriminate based on race, gender, or sexual orientation, or impose economic policies that entrench poverty while enriching the ruling class. Human rights are not regional. They are not subject to the political whims of state legislators or the biases of individual communities. They are universal, absolute, and binding upon every governing body within the nation. The ability to live free from oppression, discrimination, and state-imposed suffering shall not be dependent on geographic location. No individual shall lose fundamental protections simply by crossing a state border.

No state shall be permitted to function as an enclave of regressive ideology, crafting policies that contradict the federal guarantees of freedom and justice. No law shall allow states to enforce religious doctrine through legislation, to use morality as a justification for restricting bodily autonomy, or to create policies that disproportionately harm marginalized communities under the pretense of states' rights. The sovereignty of the people shall always supersede the sovereignty of the state, and no government, local, state, or national, shall possess the authority to determine which individuals are entitled to full personhood and which are not. States shall not serve as laboratories of oppression, testing grounds for policies that violate human rights under the guise of governance. No community shall be subjected to environmental destruction, economic deprivation, or systematic violence simply because a state legislature has determined that corporate profits, religious influence, or political control take precedence over human lives.

No state shall create, enforce, or maintain policies that restrict the right to vote, suppress participation in democratic processes, or impose artificial barriers designed to maintain political dominance. The right to vote shall not be subject to state-level restrictions that disproportionately impact marginalized communities, nor shall states be permitted to draw district lines in ways that dilute the political power of the people. Gerrymandering, voter purges, and laws that require excessive identification, proof of citizenship, or restrictions on early voting, mail-in ballots, and polling locations shall be considered direct attacks on democracy and shall be prohibited. No state shall wield its legislative power as a means of entrenching minority rule, ensuring that the outcomes of elections reflect the will of the people rather than the manipulation of political structures.

No state shall be allowed to function as a tool of economic oppression, implementing policies that prioritize corporate interests over the well-being of its citizens. The use of tax policy, land development, and labor laws to attract corporate investment at the expense of workers' rights, fair wages, and environmental protections shall be prohibited. No state shall act as a haven for exploitative businesses, permitting industries to pollute, underpay, and manipulate the labor force without consequence. The race to the bottom, in which states compete to offer the lowest wages, the weakest regulations, and the greatest benefits to corporations while denying protections to workers, shall not be allowed to continue. Economic justice shall not be undermined by the arbitrary decisions of state legislators seeking favor from industries that exploit their populations.

No state shall restrict access to healthcare, education, housing, or public resources based on economic status. The notion that access to basic necessities should depend on the wealth of an individual or the policies of their state government is an affront to the principles of justice. Healthcare is not a privilege granted by a state's budgetary priorities; it is a right. No state shall impose unnecessary restrictions on reproductive healthcare, gender-affirming medical treatment, mental health services, or lifesaving procedures under the pretense of budgetary concerns, religious morality, or political ideology. No state shall allow landlords to inflate rents unchecked, corporations to hoard housing stock, or real estate developers to price working-class families out of their own communities. The right to safe, stable housing shall not be left to the discretion of the market or to the policies of local governments willing to sacrifice their people for the benefit of wealthy investors.

Public education shall not be subject to the failures of state governance, nor shall the quality of a child's education be determined by the tax revenue of their community or the ideological preferences of state legislators. No state shall permit the defunding of public schools while diverting taxpayer money into private institutions, nor shall they rewrite history to serve political agendas. Education shall be standardized in its commitment to truth, ensuring that no child is subjected to state-sponsored misinformation, religious indoctrination, or whitewashed versions of history that erase the realities of genocide, slavery, and systemic injustice. No state shall be permitted to implement policies that criminalize students for poverty, enforce draconian disciplinary measures that disproportionately impact marginalized youth, or maintain school systems that serve as pipelines to incarceration rather than pathways to opportunity. The right to education is universal, and no state shall possess the authority to deny it through negligence, economic manipulation, or ideological obstruction.

The purpose of a nation is not to create a collection of independent power centers that prioritize their wealth, interests, and ideologies above the common good. States exist as administrative entities, not autonomous governments with the authority to undermine human rights. The role of governance is to protect, uplift, and ensure equity for all who live within its borders, not to serve as a fragmented patchwork of competing interests that leave people subject to oppression, uncertainty, and injustice based on location. No state shall exist as a law unto itself, and no government shall claim sovereignty at the expense of the people it represents. States shall not function as barriers to freedom, nor be permitted to maintain the legacy of segregation, economic disparity, or political manipulation that has long defined their role in American governance. The time for treating states as independent fiefdoms, each operating under its own rules, restrictions, and hierarchies, has ended. The time for ensuring all people, regardless of where they live, have access to the same fundamental rights, protections, and opportunities has begun.

This is not an erosion of state power, it is a reclamation of human dignity. States exist to administer governance, not dictate the terms of personhood, justice, or access to rights. No government, at any level, shall have the authority to suppress, oppress, or deny the people their freedom. The role of governance is not to hoard power but distribute it. The function of law is not to control but to protect. And the responsibility of every government, whether federal, state, or local, is to ensure that no law, policy, or ruling places the interests of those in power above the interests of the people.

Part 2: A Government That Serves or is Dismantled

Governments derive their power from the people, and when
that power is abused, when the mechanisms of governance
cease to serve the public good and instead operate as
instruments of oppression, control, and exploitation, the
people have not only the right but the obligation to dismantle
that system and build anew. No government shall exist as an
institution of wealth accumulation for the few, a fortress for
the powerful, or a vehicle for the interests of corporate
oligarchs while the majority struggle for survival. When laws
are written to shield the elite from accountability, when
institutions are designed to maintain inequality rather than
eradicate it, when policies are enacted not for justice but for
profit, that government ceases to be legitimate. The notion
that governance is a sacred structure, untouchable and
absolute, is a fabrication designed by those who benefit from
its failures. No constitution, no law, no governing body shall
hold authority that supersedes the will of the people when
that authority is wielded to entrench injustice, suppress
democracy, or uphold the dominion of Robber Barons over
the rights of the public.

The failure of a government is not marked by instability,
protests, or public discontent. It is marked by its
unwillingness to listen, adapt, and serve. No government that
perpetuates systemic corruption, corporate favoritism, or
economic feudalism shall claim to act in the name of
democracy. The function of government is to ensure the
collective well-being of its people, to protect against
exploitation, and to guarantee that no individual,

corporation, or financial institution may hoard wealth while others suffer. When politicians act as brokers for industry, when the legal system shields the rich while criminalizing the poor, when public resources are auctioned off to the highest bidder rather than allocated for the good of the many, that government has abandoned its purpose. It is not a government of the people but a cartel of power, and no such system shall be allowed to stand. Democracy does not exist in a nation where the voices of the people are drowned out by the wealth of the few, where laws are written to facilitate the privatization of the commons, where the ruling class ensures its continued dominance through policies of deliberate economic subjugation. A government that refuses to serve shall not endure.

The concentration of power in the hands of the few has never been accidental; it is the product of deliberate legal manipulation, of policies designed to protect corporate monopolies and financial empires at the expense of the working class. The Robber Barons of old never disappeared; they merely rebranded, embedding themselves into the political system, ensuring that governance itself became an extension of their power. When a government allows billionaires to shape tax policies, when it permits industries to dictate labor laws, when it enshrines corporate personhood at the expense of human dignity, it ceases to function as a government and becomes an extension of an economic ruling class. No government that serves Wall Street over workers, that prioritizes campaign donations over public welfare, that functions as an instrument of capital rather than a protector of rights, shall claim legitimacy. The rule of law is not a tool to maintain the hierarchy of the wealthy; it is a safeguard against their unchecked influence. No law shall exist that places property above people, capital above community, or corporate interests above the survival of the nation itself.

Governments that fail their people do not collapse by accident; they are brought down by their own corruption, their own excesses, their own refusal to recognize the limits of their legitimacy. No law shall grant immunity to those who commit economic crimes against the people, no legal structure shall shield those who plunder the resources of a nation while offering nothing in return. The tax codes that allow the ultra-wealthy to hoard billions while the working class is squeezed for every dollar shall be rewritten. The policies that subsidize corporate welfare while stripping social safety nets shall be abolished. The legal structures that permit wealth to accumulate in fewer and fewer hands while entire communities crumble under the weight of manufactured austerity shall not endure. The government is not a servant of industry, it is not a tool for profit; it is a collective mechanism of the people, and when it ceases to function as such, it shall be reconstructed, reclaimed, and returned to those it was meant to serve.

The right to dismantle a failing system is not radical; it is the foundation of democracy itself. The founders of this nation, however flawed in their execution, recognized that no government is eternal, that no ruling structure is immune from the necessity of revolution when it ceases to uphold the common good. The insistence that the United States must remain frozen in the legal and economic structures of past centuries, that its governing documents are unchangeable relics rather than evolving blueprints, is nothing more than the propaganda of those who benefit from the stagnation of justice. A government that exists only to sustain its own power, that refuses to adapt to the needs of its people, that clings to outdated and oppressive institutions while calling itself democracy, is no democracy at all. No document, no ruling, no tradition shall be used as an excuse for maintaining systems of oppression. No authority shall be above the scrutiny of the people. No law shall be written that serves only to uphold the status quo while millions suffer under its weight. If a government fails to evolve, to correct its injustices, to expand its protections rather than contract them, it is not a government worth preserving.

The preservation of governance is not an end in itself. The survival of a ruling system is not the same as the survival of justice. No nation shall continue simply for the sake of its own perpetuation; it shall continue only if it fulfills its role in ensuring equity, dignity, and the freedom of its people. A government that treats its citizens as expendable labor, as economic fuel for the machine of capitalism, as subjects to be controlled rather than empowered, shall not be tolerated. The policies that enrich the few at the expense of the many shall be undone. The legal structures that grant corporations more influence than citizens shall be dismantled. The institutions that were built to serve only the powerful shall be replaced with institutions that serve the people.

Governance is not a privilege for those in power; it is a responsibility to those being governed. The laws that protect wealth while criminalizing poverty, that shield corporations while abandoning the vulnerable, that enshrine privilege while denying opportunity, shall not persist. If a government does not serve the people, then the people shall take it apart and build one that does. The power of the people is absolute, and no institution, no political structure, no economic system shall stand in the way of their right to justice, to equity, to the dismantling of all that seeks to suppress them. Governance exists for the people, by the people, and when it ceases to fulfill that mandate, it shall be torn down and rebuilt in their image.

IV.
The Articles of Confederation:
No More Power Deals

Part 1: States Are Not Feudal Territories

The authority of a state shall never override the fundamental rights protected under federal law. No state shall possess the power to restrict, revoke, or manipulate individual freedoms based on regional governance, nor shall any locality impose legal barriers that deny basic human dignity. The rights of the people shall not be subject to the whims of state legislatures, nor shall geography dictate the level of justice an individual receives. Human rights are not negotiable, conditional, or dependent upon location. No state shall claim sovereignty as a means to excuse policies that infringe upon the liberties of those who reside within its borders. The purpose of a government is to ensure equality, and the function of a state is to administer governance, not to create independent power structures that erode the rights of individuals or divide a nation into territories where freedom is conditional.

The structure of governance shall ensure that no individual is denied protection, opportunity, or justice due to the policies of a particular state. No system shall exist where a person's access to healthcare, education, safety, or bodily autonomy is determined by the political majority of a state legislature. Reproductive freedom, marriage equality, gender identity recognition, and racial protections shall be uniform across all states, with no exceptions granted to those who claim that state autonomy supersedes human dignity. No state shall restrict the right to vote, limit access to polling locations, implement voter ID laws meant to suppress participation, or gerrymander districts to maintain a false majority. No local government shall impose barriers on citizens seeking medical care, gender-affirming healthcare, birth control, or abortion services. No governor, legislature, or judge shall retain the power to dictate what an individual does with their own body, whom they love, how they express their gender, or how they engage in the democratic process. The law shall be uniform in protecting these rights, and no state shall be granted the power to infringe upon them under the pretense of self-governance.

States are not feudal territories, nor shall they be treated as independent dominions within a nation that claims to protect all equally. No law shall exist that allows states to function as enclaves of corporate power, religious fundamentalism, or political control that contradicts the nation's founding principles of justice and equality. No state shall operate as a safe haven for extremist ideology, restricting the rights of women, the LGBTQ+ community, immigrants, or racial minorities under the false pretense of "moral governance." No state shall use its autonomy to justify policies that erode democracy, restrict individual freedom, or impose ideological control over its residents. No government entity shall claim that its right to exist is more important than the rights of the people it governs. The people are the foundation of a nation, not the borders, not the legislatures, not the corporate interests that seek to control policy through financial influence.

The fundamental rights of every person shall be established at the national level and enforced without exception. No state shall be permitted to segregate, discriminate, or impose legal barriers that disproportionately affect marginalized communities. No government shall pass laws designed to suppress the participation of certain groups in civic life, and no policy shall be maintained that protects the privilege of one class, race, or gender over another. The legal system shall function to ensure justice, not to uphold historical injustices through bureaucratic manipulation. The structure of governance shall not allow for the development of redlined districts, voter purges, or legal exceptions that allow discrimination to persist under the guise of state autonomy.

The economic policies of states shall not be designed to serve the wealthy while burdening the poor. No tax structure shall favor corporations at the expense of workers, and no economic incentives shall be used to extract wealth from one community while concentrating financial power in another. No state shall be permitted to function as a tax haven, allowing businesses to funnel profits through local loopholes while avoiding national accountability. The exploitation of workers shall not be protected under state labor laws, and no policy shall permit companies to pay substandard wages based on local cost-of-living arguments that ignore the broader national economy. The wealth of a state shall not be measured by the profits of corporations headquartered within its borders, but by the well-being of its people. No economic system that allows the wealthy to extract resources, labor, and land from a state while contributing nothing to its welfare shall be tolerated.

Public infrastructure, resources, and land shall not be controlled by the highest bidder. No state shall have the authority to sell public assets to private interests, nor shall any local government be permitted to privatize water, energy, or transportation in a way that places corporate profit above public welfare. No state shall serve as a testing ground for deregulation policies that permit environmental destruction, labor exploitation, or unchecked housing crises under the justification of economic growth. No system shall exist that allows wealthy individuals and corporations to buy public influence, suppress workers' rights, or control legislative outcomes through financial contributions. The legal and economic structures of a nation shall serve the people, not the industries, not the financial elite, and not the political entities that seek to consolidate power through corporate partnerships.

No legal framework shall allow states to refuse federal oversight in matters of human rights, economic justice, and environmental protection. No state shall be granted the ability to undermine national policies that ensure clean water, breathable air, sustainable development, and access to essential resources. No law shall permit local governments to ignore climate change regulations, roll back worker protections, or eliminate access to healthcare under the guise of fiscal responsibility. No community shall be forced to endure unsafe conditions, be it through pollution, food insecurity, inadequate medical services, or crumbling infrastructure, simply because the state government has chosen to prioritize corporate profit over public welfare.

The power of governance shall not be measured by the ability of states to assert dominance over their residents but by their ability to uplift, protect, and serve. No state shall use its authority to justify control, coercion, or the maintenance of outdated systems that prioritize wealth over people. The time for treating states as separate power entities that compete for resources, legislative control, and financial influence has ended. The time for ensuring that all people, regardless of where they live, have the same access to justice, opportunity, and protection has begun.

The people are the nation. The states are not independent dominions that may rule as they please, nor shall they be permitted to deny fundamental rights under the pretense of governance. No person shall be subject to policies that restrict their freedoms simply because they live within the borders of a particular state. No government shall have the authority to restrict democracy, exploit workers, or impose ideological control. The nation exists to serve its people, and no state shall have the power to dictate otherwise.

Part 2: The Purpose of a Nation is Its People, Not Its Wealth

A nation is not its corporations, its industries, or its financial markets. It is not its gross domestic product, its stock valuations, or the wealth held in private hands. A nation is its people, their well-being, their security, their freedom to live without the constant pressure of survival dictated by forces beyond their control. No government shall prioritize economic growth over human dignity, nor shall any policy be crafted that places corporate prosperity above the well-being of the population. The purpose of governance is not to facilitate wealth accumulation for the few but to ensure that all people have access to the necessities of life without fear, precarity, or exploitation. A government that measures success by the profits of industries rather than the stability and security of its citizens has failed in its most fundamental duty. The people shall not be sacrificed at the altar of economic expansion, nor shall they be treated as a disposable workforce, existing only to serve the interests of those who control capital.

No more shall states be used as tax shelters for the ultra-wealthy, granting financial havens to those who refuse to contribute to the public good. No more shall corporations be allowed to extract labor, resources, and wealth from communities without returning anything of value. No industry shall be permitted to lobby for deregulation, strip worker protections, and exploit tax loopholes while simultaneously demanding public funding, subsidies, and government bailouts. No corporation shall hold the power to dictate policy through financial coercion, nor shall any industry be granted immunity from the consequences of its exploitation. The people shall not fund the excesses of billionaires while being denied the most basic services of healthcare, education, and housing. The era of unchecked corporate influence, where industries control legislation through campaign contributions and economic threats, shall end. No company shall be permitted to amass such power that it becomes untouchable by the laws of the nation in which it profits.

A just economy does not tolerate monopolies, does not allow wealth hoarding, and does not permit industries to operate as private governments with more power than elected officials. No corporation shall be permitted to own public utilities, dictate the availability of water, or control the distribution of food, medicine, and essential goods. No company shall be allowed to manipulate markets to create artificial scarcity, inflating prices while restricting access to basic needs. No industry shall have the right to own the means of human survival, nor shall it be allowed to exploit crises for financial gain. The right to water, food, energy, and shelter shall not be conditional on income or employment status. No financial institution shall have the power to determine who may own a home, who may receive medical care, or who may access higher education. No person shall be indebted for seeking the fundamental rights necessary for survival and personal development.

The government shall serve as a force that redistributes wealth, not consolidates it. No taxation system shall be structured to benefit the wealthy at the expense of the poor. No tax loopholes shall exist that allow billionaires to evade financial responsibility while essential services remain underfunded. No subsidies shall be granted to industries that harm the public, pollute the environment, or exploit workers. No state shall operate as a financial playground for corporations seeking to minimize their tax burden while maximizing their profits. The purpose of taxation is to fund the collective good, ensuring that infrastructure, healthcare, education, and social services remain accessible to all. The wealthy shall not be shielded from financial obligation while the working class is burdened with disproportionate taxation. Those who profit the most from a nation's infrastructure, labor force, and economic stability shall contribute the most to its upkeep.

The labor of the people shall not be a resource to be extracted, controlled, and discarded at will. No economic system shall function in a way that forces people into endless cycles of work with no opportunity for rest, growth, or security. No job shall pay less than a living wage, and no industry shall exist that relies on the underpayment of workers to maintain profitability. No employer shall have the power to dictate the terms of survival, determining who may access healthcare, who may afford shelter, and who may retire with dignity. No labor force shall be treated as disposable, with workers replaced at the whims of shareholders seeking greater returns. No individual shall be denied the right to collective bargaining, to union representation, or to workplace protections that ensure safety and stability. No industry shall manipulate the economy to suppress wages, exploit temporary contracts, or outsource labor in pursuit of cheaper costs while maintaining wealth at the top. The economy shall serve the people, not the reverse.

No state shall be permitted to serve as a deregulated financial hub where corporate entities relocate to avoid national economic policies. No region shall be transformed into an economic experiment where companies test the limits of worker exploitation, environmental destruction, and consumer manipulation without oversight. No state shall be permitted to operate under financial laws that allow hedge funds, banks, and multinational corporations to move assets freely while the working class remains bound to debt and stagnant wages. No banking institution shall be permitted to create economic dependency through predatory lending, discriminatory loan policies, or interest structures designed to ensure lifelong indebtedness. The financial system shall be designed to benefit the people, ensuring that access to capital, investment, and security is distributed equitably rather than hoarded by the elite.

Public land, infrastructure, and resources shall not be sold to the highest bidder. No government shall have the authority to privatize what belongs to the people, nor shall any policy exist that allows the extraction of natural resources for private gain at the expense of public need. The transportation systems, energy grids, water supplies, and essential infrastructure of the nation shall remain under public ownership, ensuring that no company may profit by restricting access to fundamental services. No government shall allow private interests to control the development of cities, displacing communities in pursuit of profit, nor shall the financialization of housing be permitted to create cycles of eviction, speculation, and rent-seeking that make homeownership impossible for the majority. The people shall not be reduced to tenants in a country where corporations own everything. The land shall belong to those who live on it, not those who seek to control it for economic gain.

The nation does not exist to create wealth for the privileged few. It does not exist to serve corporate shareholders, private banks, or economic elites who manipulate policy for their own benefit. A government that allows its people to suffer while its industries thrive is a government that has abandoned its duty. No policy shall exist that prioritizes economic growth at the cost of human well-being. The purpose of governance is to ensure stability, justice, and prosperity for all, not to serve as an instrument of financial domination.

A nation is its people, and no economic system, no financial institution, no corporate entity shall ever hold more power than the individuals who make up its foundation. A government that fails to uphold this principle shall be dismantled, for it has already failed in its most basic purpose. The people shall not be ruled by money, nor shall they serve the interests of wealth at the expense of their own survival. The nation belongs to them, and its governance shall reflect that truth in all matters of law, policy, and economic structure.

VI.
The Amendments : What Should Have Been & What Must Be

Amendment I: The Right to a Livable Planet, Public Resources, and Food Security

The right to a habitable planet shall be guaranteed. Clean air, water, and land are fundamental human rights, protected from destruction, privatization, and corporate exploitation. No government shall permit the degradation of natural resources for profit. Ecosystem preservation shall take precedence over industrial expansion, ensuring future generations inherit a planet capable of sustaining life. Industries that pollute or harm the planet shall be dismantled. Water and essential public resources belong to the people, not corporations or financial markets. No person shall be denied clean water, nor shall any entity claim ownership for profit. Water shall be a public good, freely accessible and managed collectively. The diversion of water for profit while communities face scarcity is banned.

Food security shall not be subject to corporate manipulation, market speculation, or price inflation. No corporation shall monopolize agricultural production, patent seeds, or control food distribution for profit. Farming practices that deplete soil, contaminate water, or exploit laborers shall be abolished. Public land, including forests, rivers, and coastlines, shall remain under collective stewardship, protected for future generations. No community shall be displaced for resource extraction, and no government shall sell or transfer public lands for private gain. The production and distribution of food shall serve human need, not corporate greed.

Indigenous environmental knowledge shall be legally protected, and Indigenous stewardship of land and water recognized as essential to sustainability. No government shall sanction the displacement of Indigenous communities, nor shall corporations exploit their land without consent. Climate destruction for profit shall be recognized as a crime. The right to exist on a habitable Earth is non-negotiable.

Amendment II: The Right to Water, Land, & Public Resources

Water, land, and essential public resources shall belong to the people, not to corporations, private entities, or financial markets. No person shall be denied access to clean water, nor shall any entity claim ownership over it for profit. Water is a fundamental necessity of life and shall be protected as a public good, freely accessible and managed for the collective benefit of all. No government shall permit the privatization of water supplies, nor allow industries to extract, pollute, or hoard water resources for financial gain. The diversion of water for corporate profit while communities face scarcity shall be outlawed. No individual or community shall be forced into dependency on private companies for access to what nature provides freely.

All essential infrastructure, including energy, electricity, and transportation, shall be publicly owned and operated for the people. No corporation shall control power distribution, road maintenance, or public transit. Transportation and energy production shall serve the public good, not private wealth. No person shall be denied heat, electricity, or transportation due to financial hardship, nor shall profit-driven entities manipulate supply, inflate prices, or withhold services. The people shall not be hostage to monopolies that exploit necessity for control.

Public land, including forests, mountains, rivers, and coastlines, shall remain under collective stewardship, protected for future generations. No corporation shall claim ownership over natural landscapes, nor shall governments sell, lease, or transfer public lands for private exploitation. No person, community, or ecosystem shall be displaced for resource extraction. The nation's lands, waters, and essential services shall serve all people equally, ensuring no entity may hoard, destroy, or privatize the foundations of life itself.

Amendment III: The Right to Housing—A Nation Without the Unhoused

Housing is a fundamental right, not a privilege dictated by wealth, speculation, or corporate control. No person shall be without shelter in a society that claims to value human dignity. The government shall ensure all people have access to stable, safe, affordable housing, free from predatory financial systems that treat shelter as investment rather than necessity. No individual or family shall be displaced, evicted, or left unhoused due to poverty, systemic inequity, or profit-driven real estate practices. No law shall protect landlords or corporations extracting wealth through inflated rents while millions lack secure housing. The right to a home shall not be conditional on employment, income, or economic systems prioritizing private gain over public well-being.

No corporate entity shall own or control housing as a speculative commodity. The practice of corporate landlords accumulating vast portfolios of properties for financial manipulation, rent inflation, and artificial scarcity shall be abolished. Housing must be cooperatively or publicly owned, ensuring that communities, not financial institutions, control where people live. No person shall compete with hedge funds or foreign investors for a home. No property shall remain vacant while people sleep in the streets, and no home shall be hoarded for profit while families struggle. The right to housing means living without fear of displacement, rent hikes, or markets designed to extract wealth from those with the least.

Empty properties shall be repurposed for public use. No home shall sit unoccupied while people suffer. Governments shall seize and redistribute vacant properties held for speculation, ensuring all housing serves its intended purpose, sheltering human life. The nation shall not permit homelessness while shelter is abundant, nor shall profit ever take precedence over the basic human right to a stable home.

Amendment IV: The Right to Safety Without Unchecked Violence

The right to safety shall not be compromised by the proliferation of unchecked violence, nor shall any individual or entity possess the power to threaten, intimidate, or harm others under the guise of security. No government shall permit unregulated gun ownership, nor shall firearms be treated as commodities free from oversight. The possession, sale, and distribution of weapons shall be strictly controlled to prevent mass violence, organized intimidation, and the use of lethal force against the innocent. No individual shall be permitted to stockpile arms beyond personal necessity, and no group shall arm itself in a manner that challenges public order. The right to bear arms shall not supersede the right to live without fear of being gunned down in schools, workplaces, or public spaces.

The militarization of police and armed forces shall end. No law enforcement body shall function as an occupying force, nor shall any military-grade weaponry be deployed against the people. The use of force by police shall be subject to strict public oversight, and any officer who abuses their authority shall be held accountable by an independent civilian body. No officer shall be shielded from prosecution, and no agency shall be permitted to operate without transparency. The government shall not sanction violence under the pretense of law and order, nor shall any institution be allowed to criminalize communities for political control.

No private security force shall have authority over the public. No corporation shall employ armed personnel to police civilians, suppress dissent, or control public spaces. The use of mercenaries, paramilitary groups, or private enforcement agencies shall be prohibited. The protection of the people shall remain a public duty, accountable to the citizens it serves, ensuring that safety is not a privilege for the wealthy but a right for all.

Amendment V: The Right to Bodily Autonomy, Healthcare, and Death with Dignity

The right to bodily autonomy shall be absolute. No government, institution, or individual shall have the authority to dictate, restrict, or interfere with a person's control over their body. Reproductive freedom, including access to abortion and contraception, shall be guaranteed, protected from political, religious, or ideological interference. No law shall impose forced birth, deny medical care, or subject individuals to policies designed to strip reproductive rights. Healthcare decisions shall remain in the hands of those affected, ensuring no government wields control over private medical choices.

Healthcare shall be a fundamental right, accessible to all, without restriction due to wealth, employment, or status. No person shall be denied necessary medical treatment, nor shall life-saving care be contingent on profit, insurance, or corporate interests. No pharmaceutical company shall withhold essential medications to drive up costs, and no hospital shall deny urgent care based on financial standing. Preventative medicine, emergency care, maternal health, mental health services, and long-term treatment shall be available to all as a basic function of a just society. Medical bankruptcy shall be abolished, and no person shall face financial ruin due to illness or injury. Medicine exists for healing, not profit, and no institution shall exploit suffering.

The right to die with dignity shall be protected. No person shall be forced to endure suffering, nor shall medical intervention be denied to those who seek a humane, voluntary end to terminal illness. The government shall not interfere in end-of-life decisions, and no institution shall dictate the terms of an individual's final moments. The right to bodily autonomy extends to life and death, ensuring all people retain the agency to decide their fate, free from coercion, religious imposition, or systemic obstruction.

Amendment VI: The Right to a Just and Accountable Criminal System

Justice shall serve the people, not control them. No legal system shall exist to enforce oppression, maintain hierarchies, or criminalize poverty, race, or dissent. The death penalty shall be abolished, as no state shall have the power to take a life under the guise of justice. The prison system shall not function as a profit-driven industry, nor shall any private entity own, operate, or benefit from incarceration. No corporation shall exploit imprisoned individuals for labor, and no system shall incentivize mass incarceration. The criminal justice system shall focus on rehabilitation, restoration, and reintegration, rather than punishment and control.

No person shall be imprisoned due to wealth-based discrimination. The cash bail system, which allows the wealthy to walk free while the poor remain detained, shall be abolished. No individual shall be held in pretrial detention based on inability to pay, nor shall courts impose excessive financial penalties to maintain disparities. Three-strikes laws and mandatory minimum sentencing, which disproportionately target marginalized communities, shall be repealed. No person shall face lifelong imprisonment for nonviolent offenses, nor shall communities be subjected to laws criminalizing survival.

Community-led justice shall replace punitive policing. No law enforcement agency shall operate without public oversight, and no officer shall act with impunity. Discriminatory policing, racial profiling, and militarized law enforcement shall be prohibited. No police force shall function as an occupying military, nor shall any officer harm without consequence. Justice shall not be dictated by those who wield power but by those who demand accountability, ensuring the legal system protects, not oppresses. No system perpetuating injustice shall remain.

Amendment VII: The Right to Equal Protection Under the Law

The law shall protect all people equally, without exception or preference. No government, institution, or entity shall pass, enforce, or uphold laws that grant privileges to some while denying rights to others. No person shall be subject to discrimination based on race, gender, sexual orientation, gender identity, disability, religion, nationality, or socioeconomic status. Explicit protections shall ensure that LGBTQ+ individuals, disabled persons, and all marginalized communities are fully recognized as equal under the law, with no loopholes, exceptions, or conditional rights. No law shall diminish, restrict, or selectively apply justice based on identity, nor shall any governing body legislate morality at the expense of liberty.

Marriage equality, gender identity, and sexual orientation shall be fully recognized and protected. No state, local, or federal government shall have the authority to deny legal recognition of marriage, family structures, or identity based on religious or ideological objections. No law shall invalidate or restrict a person's right to affirm their identity, to love and marry whomever they choose, or to receive equal legal and social recognition. No institution shall impose outdated definitions of gender, sexuality, or family to justify exclusion, and no government shall strip away these rights under the guise of protecting so-called traditional values.

Religious exemptions shall not override human rights. No faith, doctrine, or belief system shall grant legal permission to discriminate, nor shall any institution claim the right to deny services, employment, medical care, or recognition to any person based on religious convictions. Freedom of religion shall not be used as a tool for oppression. The law shall serve all people equally, ensuring that justice, dignity, and civil rights are not contingent on religious doctrine but on the universal and inalienable rights of all individuals.

Amendment VIII: The Right to Labor Protections & Economic Security

The economy shall serve the people, not the reverse. No individual shall accumulate wealth to the detriment of society, and no billionaire shall exist in a system where poverty remains. Extreme wealth shall be recognized as an economic failure, a distortion of justice, and a concentration of power that undermines democracy. Monopolies, corporate domination, and unchecked financial hoarding shall be abolished. No company, industry, or institution shall hold such influence that it dictates government policy, suppresses competition, or exploits the labor of the many for the benefit of the few. Wealth shall be distributed equitably, ensuring that no person is forced into poverty while others amass fortunes beyond necessity.

Businesses beyond a certain size shall be worker-owned. No corporation shall function as an empire under the control of a single person, family, or elite class. Decisions about labor, production, and wages shall be made democratically by those who contribute their time and effort, not by distant executives concerned only with profit. The right to unionize shall be absolute, and no employer shall interfere in the collective bargaining process. No person shall be subject to exploitative wages, unsafe conditions, or employment structures that offer no stability or benefits. The economy shall be built on cooperation, not exploitation, ensuring that workers retain control over the value they create.

Universal basic income shall guarantee that no person is forced into poverty. No individual shall be denied food, shelter, or dignity due to financial hardship. The right to exist shall not be contingent on participation in a labor market that extracts more than it provides. Economic security shall be guaranteed for all, ensuring that wealth is a shared resource, not a tool for oppression. No system built on economic enslavement shall be permitted to endure.

Amendment IX: The Right to a Decentralized Economy & Public Control of Currency

The control of money shall rest with the people, not private interests, financial elites, or centralized institutions that manipulate economies for profit. No corporation, bank, or entity shall hold exclusive power over the issuance, valuation, or distribution of currency. The creation and regulation of money shall be a public function, ensuring that economic stability serves the collective good rather than wealth accumulation. No private institution shall have the authority to inflate, devalue, or restrict access to currency in ways that disproportionately benefit the elite while destabilizing communities. Artificial scarcity, speculative hoarding, and financial manipulation shall be outlawed. No government shall bail out private financial institutions while leaving the people to suffer the consequences of crises created by reckless profit-seeking.

A decentralized economy shall replace centralized financial control. No single governing body or corporate interest shall dictate the terms of commerce, trade, or exchange. Communities shall have the right to establish alternative economic systems that reflect their needs, ensuring that trade is not solely dictated by fiat currency controlled by a central authority. Barter, cooperative exchange, and community-based currencies shall be recognized as legitimate, ensuring economic participation is not restricted by centralized financial power. No law shall prohibit the right of individuals to engage in direct trade, mutual aid, or financial arrangements outside traditional banking systems.

The economy shall serve people, not profit-driven institutions. No financial system shall be permitted to trap individuals in debt, control wealth for private gain, or dictate the conditions of survival. Economic sovereignty shall belong to the people, ensuring that currency facilitates trade and prosperity, not economic hierarchies.

Amendment X: The Right to Self-Governance & Direct Democracy

The power to govern shall rest with the people, not political elites, corporations, or financial interests. No government shall exist as a separate ruling class, detached from those it serves. Governance shall be transparent, participatory, and directly accountable, ensuring that policies, budgets, and decisions reflect the will of the people rather than the influence of private wealth. No individual, party, or institution shall dictate policy through financial control, nor shall elections function as competitions of wealth, where those with the most resources hold disproportionate influence over governance. The era of corporate-sponsored democracy shall end, replaced by a system in which public interest, not money, determines leadership and policy.

All elections shall be publicly funded. No candidate shall accept corporate money, dark money, or private donations, and no election shall be influenced by wealth disparities. Political campaigns shall operate on equal financial footing, ensuring that access to leadership is not reserved for the rich. No political advertisement shall be funded by private interests, and no lobbying group shall hold greater sway than the voice of a single voter. The right to self-governance shall not be compromised by a system where elections can be bought, and policies can be sold.

The people shall vote directly on major policies through publicly owned technology. No law, budget, or decision affecting the public shall be made without public consent. Government budgets shall be fully transparent, with all expenditures publicly available and subject to citizen approval. No official shall act in secrecy, and no governing body shall shield itself from public accountability. Democracy shall be direct, digital, and universally accessible, ensuring that governance reflects the will of the people in real-time, without manipulation, delay, or obstruction.

Amendment XI: The Right to Lifelong Education

Education shall be a fundamental right, freely accessible from birth to death, ensuring that all individuals, regardless of economic status, have the opportunity to develop their potential and contribute to society. No person shall be denied access to learning due to financial hardship, nor shall education be treated as a commodity available only to those who can afford it. All levels of education, from early childhood to higher education, trade schools, and continuing education, shall be publicly funded, eliminating financial barriers that have long restricted opportunity. The burden of student debt shall be abolished, and no institution shall profit from the pursuit of knowledge. No person shall be forced into lifelong financial hardship for learning, nor shall access to education be contingent on wealth, privilege, or institutional gatekeeping.

Trade schools, apprenticeships, and alternative education programs shall be funded equally alongside traditional academic institutions, ensuring that education is not limited to a single pathway. No person shall be forced into a career based on economic necessity rather than personal aptitude or interest, and no one shall be trapped in an industry with no means of retraining or skill development. Lifelong education shall be guaranteed, allowing individuals to pursue new fields, adapt to technological advancements, and engage in intellectual growth at any stage of life. No government shall restrict access to education, nor shall institutions be permitted to censor knowledge to serve political or ideological control.

Education shall exist to empower, enlighten, and uplift, not to generate profit or reinforce social hierarchies. A just society requires informed citizens, and the right to learn shall remain protected, ensuring that knowledge is freely shared, never hoarded, commodified, or controlled by those in power.

Amendment XII: The Right to Arts, Culture, and Community Spaces

The right to art, culture, and communal spaces shall be protected as essential to human expression, identity, and social well-being. No government or corporation shall restrict public access to cultural resources, nor shall artistic expression be dictated by profit. Public funding shall ensure that the arts, including music, literature, theater, and visual expression, remain accessible to all. No person shall be denied the ability to create, share, or experience art due to economic status, and no institution shall profit from restricting cultural enrichment. Libraries, museums, and artistic institutions shall remain fully funded and publicly owned, ensuring that knowledge and creativity are available to all, not commodities controlled by private interests.

No community shall be displaced in the name of economic development. Gentrification, the systematic erasure of historically significant neighborhoods for corporate profit, shall be prohibited. No cultural space, artistic district, or community landmark shall be demolished, privatized, or repurposed in ways that exclude those who built and sustained them. Public investment in cultural preservation shall take priority over commercial development, ensuring that no group is stripped of its artistic, historical, or communal identity for financial gain.

Civic centers, public parks, and free gathering spaces shall remain accessible to all. No person shall be excluded from shared spaces due to economic status, and no entity shall privatize land intended for public use. Community spaces shall serve as places for education, activism, and cultural expression, ensuring that all people have access to environments where creativity, dialogue, and connection can flourish. The right to belong in public spaces shall not be dictated by wealth, privilege, or profit.

Amendment XIII: The Right to Time & Work-Life Balance

Time is not a privilege of the wealthy but a fundamental right of all people. No society that values human dignity shall force individuals to sacrifice their health, family, or well-being to survive. No government shall allow an economic system that requires people to work multiple jobs just to afford basic necessities, nor shall any employer be permitted to exploit labor by denying fair wages, benefits, or humane working conditions. Work shall exist to support life, not consume it.

A four-day workweek shall be the standard, ensuring that no person is required to surrender the majority of their waking hours to labor while having no time for rest, relationships, or personal fulfillment. Productivity shall not be measured by hours worked but by the quality of life it provides. Mandatory paid vacation, parental leave, and sick leave shall be guaranteed for all workers, regardless of industry or employment status. No employer shall deny time off for caregiving, illness, or personal well-being, and no person shall be forced to choose between their health and their livelihood. No government shall permit an economy where exhaustion is the norm, and leisure is a luxury only for the privileged.

No individual shall work under conditions that strip them of autonomy, stability, or security. Wages shall ensure a dignified life, and no job shall exist that leaves workers in poverty. Economic systems shall be structured to provide for human needs, not corporate profits. The right to time shall be protected as fiercely as any other right, ensuring that life is not reduced to endless labor, but lived fully, with dignity, rest, and balance. No government shall permit an economy that values profits over people.

Amendment XIV: The Right to Rest & Aging with Dignity

A society that values human life must honor the right to rest and ensure that aging is met with dignity, care, and security. No person shall be forced to work until death due to financial insecurity, nor shall retirement be a privilege reserved for the wealthy. Guaranteed retirement income shall be provided to all, ensuring that no individual who has contributed to society is abandoned to poverty in old age. No government shall permit an economy where the elderly are left struggling to afford housing, food, or healthcare, nor shall corporations be allowed to erode pension systems or siphon away retirement funds for profit. Financial security in old age shall be a fundamental right, not a gamble dictated by market fluctuations or employment history.

Elder care shall be recognized as a public responsibility, not a private burden. No person shall be denied long-term care, assisted living, or in-home support due to financial status. Public funding shall guarantee that aging individuals receive necessary medical attention, housing, and social support without relying on family members forced to sacrifice their own stability. No healthcare system shall be structured to neglect the elderly, and no profit-driven institution shall exploit aging populations for financial gain.

No person shall be coerced into working beyond their physical, mental, or emotional capacity. Forced productivity past retirement age shall be prohibited, and no government shall mandate policies that pressure the elderly to remain in the workforce to survive. Rest is a right, not a luxury. A just society ensures that those who have labored throughout life are given the peace, security, and care they deserve, without fear of financial ruin, neglect, or forced work in their final years.

Amendment XV: The Right to Privacy & Data Ownership

Privacy is a fundamental right, and no government, corporation, or entity shall have the authority to collect, store, exploit, or sell personal data without explicit, informed consent. No individual's digital identity, communications, or personal information shall be treated as a commodity, nor shall data be harvested, manipulated, or analyzed for profit, surveillance, or control. The right to privacy shall extend to all technology, ensuring no person is subjected to unwarranted tracking, profiling, or data mining. No government shall permit mass collection of personal information under the guise of security, nor shall any corporation be granted legal authority to extract, sell, or trade an individual's digital footprint for financial gain.

All people shall have full ownership of their personal data, including the right to control, delete, and restrict access to any information collected about them. No company, platform, or institution shall claim ownership over an individual's online presence, activity, or digital communications. The right to erase data, revoke consent, and refuse participation in digital tracking shall be absolute, ensuring that privacy is not merely a conditional privilege granted by service providers, but a protected and inalienable right. No law shall force individuals to surrender personal data in exchange for access to public services, employment, or social participation.

Governments shall be prohibited from engaging in mass surveillance without just cause and due process. The use of artificial intelligence, facial recognition, biometric tracking, and predictive policing shall be subject to strict legal oversight, ensuring that privacy is not eroded under the pretense of technological advancement. No society that values freedom shall permit the digital exploitation of its people, nor shall privacy be sacrificed for corporate or governmental convenience.

Amendment XVI: The Right to Protection from AI &
Automation Abuse

Artificial intelligence and automation shall serve humanity,
not exploit, displace, or control it. No government,
corporation, or institution shall deploy AI in ways that
undermine dignity, replace human labor without economic
security, or concentrate power in the hands of the few. No
individual shall be denied employment, healthcare, housing,
or due process based on automated decision-making systems
without oversight or accountability. AI shall not enforce
economic or social hierarchies, nor be used to reinforce
systemic discrimination under the guise of neutrality. The
development and application of artificial intelligence shall be
subject to strict public regulation, ensuring it remains a tool
for human advancement rather than exploitation.

Automation must serve people, not displace them. No
company shall replace human workers with machines solely
to increase profits while abandoning those who built their
industries. The implementation of automation shall require
corresponding protections for affected workers, including
guaranteed retraining, economic support, and equitable
redistribution of productivity gains. No government shall
subsidize the development of AI that eliminates jobs without
ensuring social safety nets and protections for displaced
workers. The right to work shall not be sacrificed for
corporate efficiency, nor shall technological progress be used
as an excuse to strip people of their livelihoods.

All AI-driven decisions in hiring, healthcare, policing, and
housing shall be fully transparent, with clear accountability
and human oversight. No automated system shall have the
final authority over life-altering outcomes, and no black-box
algorithms shall dictate the distribution of resources, services,
or rights. AI shall exist to augment human potential, not
diminish it, ensuring that technology remains a servant of the
people rather than their replacement or oppressor.

114

Amendment XVII: The Right to Indigenous Sovereignty &
Environmental Protection

Indigenous nations shall be sovereign, with all rights to self-governance, land stewardship, and cultural preservation protected under the law. No government, corporation, or institution shall infringe upon Indigenous autonomy, nor shall historical treaties be ignored or dismissed. The legal obligations of the United States to Indigenous nations shall be upheld without exception, ensuring past injustices are addressed through enforceable treaty rights, land restoration, and reparative measures. No law, policy, or development project shall override Indigenous sovereignty, and no government shall claim authority over Indigenous land, resources, or governance. The right of Indigenous peoples to determine their future, laws, and societal structures shall be absolute, free from federal, state, or corporate interference.

Land restoration shall be recognized as a legal and moral obligation. No government or private entity shall be permitted to extract, exploit, or desecrate land taken through colonial expansion, forced removal, or broken treaties. Restoration of sacred sites, natural resources, and historical lands shall be mandated, ensuring that Indigenous communities have the full right to reclaim, protect, and sustain the lands stolen from them. Environmental protection shall follow Indigenous stewardship principles, recognizing that the health of the planet is inseparable from the rights of those who have safeguarded it for generations. No policy shall allow corporate destruction of ecosystems, water sources, or biodiversity at the expense of future generations.

The ecological future of the nation shall be determined not by corporate greed but by Indigenous knowledge and sustainable practices. No government shall prioritize short-term economic gain over environmental survival, and no law shall override the inherent right of Indigenous peoples to protect the land, air, and water for all.

Amendment XVIII: The Right to Migration & Refugee Protections

Migration is a fundamental human right, and no person shall be criminalized for seeking safety, stability, or a better life. No government shall deny entry, asylum, or refuge to those fleeing war, climate disasters, political persecution, or systemic violence. No nation shall build barriers to survival, nor shall any law be used to dehumanize, detain, or punish those forced to migrate due to conditions beyond their control. Borders shall not serve as instruments of exclusion, and no individual shall be subjected to imprisonment, forced displacement, or separation from their families for exercising their right to move in search of protection.

The United States shall abolish border detention centers and all policies that separate families, imprison asylum seekers, or deny due process to those seeking refuge. No child shall be held in cages, no family shall be torn apart, and no asylum seeker shall be criminalized for seeking protection. The detention and deportation of migrants for profit shall be outlawed, and no government agency or private entity shall benefit from the imprisonment or exploitation of displaced people. Asylum and refugee processes shall be fair, humane, and accessible, ensuring that no person is left stateless, imprisoned, or forced into dangerous conditions due to bureaucratic cruelty or political agendas.

Immigration policy shall be rooted in human dignity, not nationalism, economic exploitation, or racial discrimination. No person shall be denied basic rights based on documentation status, and all people residing within the nation shall have access to healthcare, education, and legal protections. The right to migrate shall be respected as part of global human freedom, ensuring that those seeking safety are met with compassion, not hostility, incarceration, or exclusion.

Amendment XIX: The Right to Dismantle Any System That Fails the People

No government, institution, or law shall be upheld as sacred if it harms the people. No system shall exist for its own preservation at the expense of justice, dignity, or human rights. The legitimacy of governance is not derived from longevity, tradition, or the power of those in control, but from its ability to serve the people fairly, equitably, and without oppression. When any institution, whether political, economic, or legal, ceases to function for the collective good and instead perpetuates harm, inequality, or exploitation, the people shall have the absolute right to dismantle, reform, or replace it. The right to abolish failing systems is not rebellion; it is the foundation of self-governance and a necessary safeguard against tyranny.

The Constitution shall not be treated as an unchangeable artifact but as a living document meant to evolve with the needs of the people. No law, precedent, or institution shall be immune to challenge, revision, or dissolution if it fails to uphold justice. The people, not the ruling class, shall determine when a system has outlived its usefulness or become corrupted beyond repair. Legal and political structures shall not be barriers to progress but tools for justice, subject to continuous scrutiny and correction.

If a government no longer serves the people but instead exists to sustain wealth, power, or elite control, it shall be dismantled. If laws are written to protect those in power rather than those they govern, they shall be void. The people's right to shape their society, their institutions, and their future shall be absolute, ensuring that governance remains a reflection of justice, not an enforcer of oppression.

Amendment XX: The Right to Collective Ownership of Innovation and Knowledge

No corporation or individual shall claim ownership over technologies essential to public welfare, including medical advancements, agricultural innovations, and climate solutions. Intellectual property laws shall prioritize human need over profit, ensuring lifesaving medicines, green technologies, and critical knowledge remain public. No person shall be denied healthcare, sustainable energy, or essential information due to patent restrictions or monopolization. Public research institutions shall receive funding to develop and distribute innovations equitably, ensuring progress benefits society.

Scientific and technological advancements shall serve humanity, not private wealth accumulation. The privatization of essential research, the hoarding of patents for profit, and the suppression of public access to critical discoveries shall be prohibited. The development of pharmaceuticals, vaccines, renewable energy, and food security innovations shall be funded and shared in ways that benefit all people rather than a select few. No essential discovery shall be withheld to manipulate markets, and no government shall grant corporations the unchecked authority to dictate the cost of survival or technological progress.

Open-source, community-driven innovation shall be legally protected, ensuring that knowledge and discoveries remain accessible to all rather than enriching a privileged few. No law shall allow corporations to restrict access to essential medical treatments, climate technologies, or scientific research in ways that disadvantage the public. Educational and research institutions shall be required to share critical knowledge without restrictive licensing. The advancement of society shall be guided by collective well-being, not the financial interests of monopolies, ensuring that progress is a right, not a privilege.

In Summary:
A Constitution for Liberation, Finally

A Constitution for Liberation: The United States Reimagined for Women in 2025

The Constitution of the United States of America and Founding Documents Reimagined for Women 2025 seeks to correct the systemic injustices embedded in the original founding documents by centering justice, equality, and dignity for women and all marginalized communities. This reimagined constitution is not a mere revision but a fundamental restructuring that recognizes the failures of the past and establishes a legal foundation for a just society.

This document ensures that no law, institution, or system exists solely to preserve power for the few at the expense of the many. It prioritizes the well-being of the people over profit, dismantles oppressive hierarchies, and guarantees that governance serves those who have been historically excluded.

Articles of Governance

The revised Constitution is structured into distinct articles that redefine governance, representation, and accountability to the people.

- Article I: The People's Assembly – Establishes direct democracy, where governance is a collective process rather than a tool of political elites.

- Article II: Representation Without Oppression – Abolishes corporate influence, guarantees equal representation, and ensures leadership reflects the people.

- Article III: Judicial Reform and Abolition of Injustice – Ends mass incarceration, eliminates for-profit prisons, and enforces true accountability within the justice system.

- Article IV: The Economic Framework for Equality – Shifts the economy from a system of exploitation to one of collective ownership and wealth distribution.

- Article V: Rights of Women and Marginalized Genders – Codifies reproductive freedom, bodily autonomy, and absolute legal equality.

- Article VI: The End of White Supremacy and Patriarchy in Law – Eliminates legal structures that uphold racial, gender, and economic hierarchies.

- Article VII: Environmental and Indigenous Justice – Declares environmental protection and Indigenous sovereignty as central to governance.

- Article VIII: The Abolition of Militarized Policing and Surveillance – Disarms police, bans mass surveillance, and replaces punitive policing with community-led justice.

- Article IX: The Protection of Culture, Knowledge, and Education – Guarantees free and accessible education, protects artistic and cultural expression, and ends corporate control over information.

- Article X: A Living Constitution for a Just Future – Ensures no law or institution is immutable if it fails to serve the people, affirming the right to dismantle systems of oppression.

Bill of Rights Reimagined: 20 Amendments for Liberation

The amendments establish explicit rights ensuring that governance serves the people, not the powerful.

1. The Right to a Livable Planet, Public Resources, and Food Security – Guarantees environmental protection,

public ownership of water and land, and the abolition of corporate-controlled food systems.

2. The Right to Water, Land, and Public Resources – Prohibits the privatization of natural resources and public services, ensuring collective ownership of essential goods.

3. The Right to Housing: A Nation Without the Unhoused – Declares housing a human right, abolishes corporate real estate speculation, and guarantees stable, affordable homes for all.

4. The Right to Safety Without Unchecked Violence – Ends unregulated gun ownership, disarms police, and prohibits the militarization of law enforcement.

5. The Right to Bodily Autonomy, Healthcare, and Death with Dignity – Protects reproductive freedom, establishes universal healthcare, and legalizes end-of-life choices.

6. The Right to a Just and Accountable Criminal System – Abolishes the death penalty, eliminates cash bail, and replaces punitive policing with restorative justice.

7. The Right to Equal Protection Under the Law – Ensures legal recognition and full protections for LGBTQ+ individuals, disabled persons, and all marginalized communities.

8. The Right to Labor Protections and Economic Security – Abolishes billionaires, mandates worker-owned businesses, and guarantees a universal basic income.

9. The Right to a Decentralized Economy and Public Control of Currency – Ends private control over money, abolishes financial manipulation, and legalizes community-based economies.

10.   The Right to Self-Governance and Direct Democracy – Establishes publicly owned voting technology, ends corporate-funded elections, and mandates transparent government budgets.

11.   The Right to Lifelong Education – Guarantees free education from birth to death, abolishes student debt, and funds trade schools and apprenticeships.

12.   The Right to Arts, Culture, and Community Spaces – Ensures public funding for the arts, protects cultural spaces from gentrification, and preserves free gathering places.

13.   The Right to Time and Work-Life Balance – Establishes a four-day workweek, mandates paid leave, and ensures no one is forced to work multiple jobs to survive.

14.   The Right to Rest and Aging with Dignity – Guarantees retirement income, public elder care, and bans forced productivity past retirement age.

15.   The Right to Privacy and Data Ownership – Ends corporate surveillance, protects digital identities, and ensures personal data is not a commodity.

16.   The Right to Protection from AI and Automation Abuse – Prevents AI from replacing human dignity, ensures technology serves people rather than displacing them, and mandates full transparency in automated decision-making.

17.   The Right to Indigenous Sovereignty and Environmental Protection – Recognizes Indigenous nations as sovereign, mandates land restoration, and follows Indigenous environmental stewardship principles.

18.   The Right to Migration and Refugee Protections – Abolishes border detention centers, protects those fleeing war and climate disasters, and guarantees the right to seek safety without criminalization.

19.   The Right to Dismantle Any System That Fails the People – Declares that no government, law, or institution is sacred if it harms the people, affirming the right to revolution when justice is denied.

20.   The Right to Public Knowledge and Open Innovation – Ensures essential technologies, medical advancements, and climate solutions remain public, prioritizing collective benefit over profit.

A Constitution That Serves the People

This reimagined Constitution corrects the foundational failures of the original document, which prioritized the interests of wealthy white men while codifying the oppression of women, Indigenous peoples, and the working class. The Founding Fathers designed a system where power remained concentrated in the hands of a few, where wealth dictated access to justice, and where violence was sanctioned to maintain control. That system has endured through centuries, morphing to accommodate the capitalist interests of corporations, billionaires, and political elites while leaving the majority struggling.

This Constitution abolishes that system. It refuses to accept that governance must be built on exploitation and control. It reclaims democracy, labor, and land from those who have hoarded power for generations and redistributes them to the people who sustain society.

Governance must be participatory. Leadership must reflect the communities it serves. No law is immutable if it perpetuates suffering. The economy must be designed to ensure security, not extract wealth from the most vulnerable. Justice must mean liberation, not punishment.

Women, long relegated to the margins of law and policy, take their rightful place as central architects of this new governance. Reproductive freedom is non-negotiable. Economic security is guaranteed. Safety is redefined as protection from systemic violence rather than policing that serves the elite. The land and water are restored to public ownership, and environmental destruction for corporate gain is criminalized.

This document is a rejection of oppression, a blueprint for a world in which governance serves all people, and a declaration that no system that fails its people deserves to stand. It is not just a correction. It is a revolution.

Conclusion
A Nation that Belongs to the Living

The first Constitution was a contract with power, not with people. It was drafted by men who saw equality as a threat, who built loopholes into the foundation, who enshrined their own supremacy in ink and called it freedom. They did not write a nation for all, they wrote a fortress for themselves, leaving the rest to scale the walls or perish outside them.

The Declaration of Independence was a declaration of dominance. The Articles of Confederation were a handshake among rulers. The Bill of Rights was a concession to control, granting just enough to quiet rebellion while ensuring the architects of oppression would never lose their throne. These documents were never sacred. They were scaffolding for an empire built on exclusion.

Now, they are rewritten. Not softened. Not tempered. Torn from their foundations and rebuilt with justice as the only law. The echoes of the past are gone. The rot is burned away. There is no place left for those who still kneel before the ghosts of dead men.

This is the reckoning.

About the author

The author live removed.

Please feel free to burn part or all of this book, safely, as an effigy.

www.ingramcontent.com/pod-product-compliance
Lightning Source LLC
Chambersburg PA
CBHW021623270326
41931CB00008B/840